Martin Luther King in the African American Preaching Tradition

Martin Luther King

IN THE
AFRICAN AMERICAN
PREACHING TRADITION

Valentino
Lassiter

WIPF & STOCK · Eugene, Oregon

Wipf and Stock Publishers
199 W 8th Ave, Suite 3
Eugene, OR 97401

Martin Luther King in the African American Preaching Tradition
By Lassiter, Valentino
Copyright©2001 Pilgrim Press
ISBN 13: 978-1-60899-564-6
Publication date 4/19/2010
Previously published by Pilgrim Press, 2001

CONTENTS

PREFACE

Cast your bread upon the waters, for after many days you will
find it agin.
                    —ECCLESISTES 11:1 (New International Version)

THIS BOOK IS A NOBLE ENDEAVOR to comprise a concise compari-
son of the historic spiritual tradition of dynamic African American preaching and the gifted preaching nature of Martin Luther
King Jr. The study details the central importance of the preaching legacy within African American religious culture from the
earliest colonial Biblical lections by slave preachers, to the more
dignified, yet spiritually powerful presentation of twentieth century scholar-preachers as exemplified by King. At the right time,
our hearts and our ears were trained to hear Martin Luther King
as that of a unique prophetic voice. At the same time, an important truth lies in the fact that this blessed and God-commissioned
preacher was a product and an extension of a tradition of preaching voices that have upheld and encouraged the lives of the people
since the early 1600s.

Preaching in the African American tradition remains a most
important element of the worship experience. Other factions of
gathered *Koinonia* or *Sacred Community* only give rise to the sermonic moment. The people of God, there so gathered, sit in anticipation to learn just what the Word is saying for the day. The
songs of Zion also did, indeed, speak to the soul. The loving fel-

lowship of kindred spirits is very significant. Yet, the momentous spiritual event occurs in that special place and time as the person of God expounds upon life-sustaining truths and spiritual suggestions with a keen sense of theological soundness. As a result of the casting of these arrays of "spiritual breads" upon the "waters" of living and everyday survival, persons are empowered to envision fresh possibilities and new visions for "many days." There is no moment so glorious for spirit seekers as that moment of the preached Word. This is the time to turn "all" to the Being and to truly hear from "heaven." There is great probability that many arrive at the sacred space with a deep sense of "hunger" for this bread. Such existential anticipation leads to an hour of powerful interaction of mind, imagination, hope, and destiny. The skilled preacher of the culture has been able to connect difficult and uncertain worldly struggles to an indubitable hope and patterns of engaging survival.

I am suggesting that long before the genesis of the African American theological academy, spiritually skilled orality was the essence of life-based truths that were reliant upon a God that was perceived as a God of universal justice. Not only was this distinctive genre of preaching divergent in character of style, sound, and theological interpretation, but the very reception by the adherents was special. Further, I purport that the very content of African American preaching hermeneutics has remained focused on four major premises from slavery to the present.

First, the God of African American worship has always been and will remain the unquestionable sustainer of the world. In this activity of divine omnipotence, God remains a God of indivisible justice. Second, the world not only maintains a well-defined *physical* order; but there also exists a permanent *moral* order as well. "Right" is always sure to reign over evil. Third, it does not matter how truculent or how externally uncertain the cosmos may become as a result of either human actions or divine deeds that may have far-reaching consequences. The Sustained and Gracious One is yet loving, caring, powerful, and remains in *full* control of the cosmos. And last, in all situations, there exists a divine sense of unquestionable ability (i.e., "God is able"). This sense of divine jurisdiction is not without an extension of grace and mercy (i.e., "God is good").

These four premises suggest the major theological genre and content of sermonic expression and assumptions on which African American preaching is historically grounded. Such ideals represent the major theological content and postulations of the spoken worship experience. Further, I would argue that these four premises also have historically conditioned the faith expectations of the gathered community.

MUSICAL SERMONS AND STYLES OF PRESENTATION

A very crucial companion to the African American preaching heritage is the theology inherent in Negro Spirituals. These songs presented emotional constructs of ontology that continue to hold lasting hermeneutical effects. Moreover, these musical events helped to shape and to tenor the message of the slave preacher. Such expressions of deep-spirited disorientation, as well as those songs of renewed focus and determination, provided very important content that became the corpus of early African American theological discourse. Such musical hermeneutical constructs addressed such vital issues as:

- Strong use of biblical personalities
- The cosmos
- Protest to the slavery institution
- Lament for detached family members
- Depressive statements regarding ongoing ill-defined humanity
- Hope for better times
- Steadfast determination in the struggle
- The assurance of a just God, who willed freedom for all

African American preaching hermeneutics have centered on such themes of this nature at all times. From the days of colonial slavery and the Society of the Propagation of the Gospel to the present, the message remains focused on human survival.

TWENTIETH-CENTURY PREACHING AND MARTIN LUTHER KING JR.

From the Invisible Institution[1] to the days of institutional African American worship houses, the urging and calling of preachers remained paramount in the cultural development and in the historical destiny of African Americans. Preaching continued to hold very important implications for social transitions and identity. At the turn of the century, the African American church remained the major prophetic voice of the community. The church provided a number of important roles and services that were not open to African Americans by other public and private institutions. Hence, worship and preaching were important aspects of social as well as spiritual life. The transitional role of preaching remained of vital importance during the various stages of racial and social challenge.

The 1950s served as a very critical testing ground to demonstrate the importance of spiritually directed vocal dialogue. Moreover, a crucial prophetic voice of the African American preacher is heard over the horizon of a country that faces racial, moral, and spiritual crisis. Enter a young minister with a Boston University doctorate, back to his native South where racism and Jim Crow were still rampant. In Montgomery, Alabama, as in most southern cities, laws upheld the privilege of whites to claim first choice to the better, upper seating on public transportation. Of course, law also held that if blacks did manage to grasp a seat in the rear of the coaches, they were to surrender them at the request of whites.

We recall that a hardworking seamstress by the name of Rosa Parks decided on December 1, 1955, that a "first-come first-served" policy was long overdue and that a D-day on segregation should be declared. The town, of course, responded in shock. The "Negro" community organized within their only controlled and owned space, the church. On December 5 of that same week, King was elected to head this new revolutionary protest group that fostered religious implications. There, at the Holt Street Baptist Church, where the Montgomery Improvement Association held nightly meetings to encourage each other during this citywide bus boycott, a young Rev. Dr. Martin Luther King Jr., night after night, electrified the protesting audience with spiritual encouragement and theo-political musings. A new prophet had been called and a "movement" of revolutionary status had begun.

During the movement, King evolved as a great leader, a prolific teacher of nonviolent protest, and a celebrated preacher of the gospel of peace and freedom. He employed organizing techniques of outstanding nature. In addition, his spoken directives and sermonic pedagogy made him one of the most influential leaders and preachers of the century. Skilled with Tillichian cogitation, Hegelian sagacity, Niebuhrian principles, and potent Christological truths, King yet remained a preacher who was particular in wisdom and universal in effectiveness.

In this process, there arose a very radical but Bible-based gospel of nonviolent resistance and love. King celebrated the tradition of African American preaching in his effectively delineated writings as well as in his dynamic orality. In the process of reciting and rehearsing the perceived prophetic acts of a God of justice and, at the same time, fostering hopeful images of eschatological peace, King lifted the sights of many who previously were unable to imagine freedom. Moreover, his preaching style of the native African American church served as a sounding "drum" to move the church into eras of new courage and unrealized possibility.

African American traditional preaching faces the challenge of different drums that echo the same ancient message. Contemporary styles of worship and preaching press us to examine the different approaches to the spoken word that is yet very important for direction, empowerment, and ongoing spiritual identity. This text will examine these challenges and suggest ongoing tasks for effective preaching.

CHAPTER ONE

EARLY CASTINGS

*Primitive Forms and Constructs of the
African American Preaching Tradition*

IS THERE ANY WORD FROM THE LORD? This question which was deep in the souls of slaves who sought spiritual personhood still rings in the hearts of African American worshipers today. For many, other elements of worship are only preliminary to the preached word. This confirms the importance and centrality that preaching has held in African American worship from the Invisible Institution to the present.

The power of the preached word remains a very high priority in African American worship. The singing of very involving gospel choirs is often uplifting. Testimonies of weekly spiritual journeys may be shared and related by "testifying" individuals to a listening sympathetic congregation. Yet, there is no moment so glorious for the gathered worshipers as the moment of the preached word. This is the time to truly turn "all" to the "Being" and to "hear from heaven." The preceding anticipation of spirit leads to this hour of powerful interaction of mind, imagination, hope, and destiny. The skilled and consecrated preacher is able to connect difficult and uncertain worldly struggle to clear, indubitable hope and patterns for survival. He/she is in a special position to present worshipers an unrivaled sense of hope and efficacious worldview.

As many other students of this African American folk preaching tradition, Martin Luther King Jr. felt a deep loyalty to this style of spiritual oratory. Upon reaching levels of accord with the masses, he seldom deviated from the basic form of African American folk preaching. This text will demonstrate the fact that his intellect and superb theological training were assets that gave his preaching a mysterious quality. This combination, of course, heralded him as one of the world's greatest preacher/theologians of the twentieth century.

Let us now examine this celebrated history of African American preaching. The spirited forms and content of this tradition have been an impetus for justice and identity throughout the history of African Americans in this country. Moreover, these colorful hermeneutics and dynamic delivery of the good news has deep roots in African religion and in early Afro-Christian expressions during the colonial period of this country.

AFRICAN ORAL RELIGIOUS TRADITIONS

Historically, theology in the African American folk tradition has been an oral phenomenon. Generations of pulpiteers have shared many of these skills of vocal delivery, thought, and ideals that have remained a part of the sacred oral culture. A lack of many literary forms of religious expression has made necessary a very unique and lasting oral tradition of religious preservation and definitions. From the ceremonial chants and language of the *iya-ilu* motherdrum of the Yoruba Dundas,[1] to the worship of slaves, to the modern-known revival greats as Cesar Clark, Yvonne Delk, and Gardner Taylor, we get a deep appreciation of the importance of oral transmission through the black preaching experience.

It is important to note that the cultural roots of African American preaching (unlike studies in sacred music) have not long been a subject of scholastic study. Experts of homiletics and hermeneutics have brought to our attention many new insights into this area. Included in this category are scholars such as Henry Mitchell, Stephen B. Reid, Charles Hamilton, and many others who have examined this area of theological study. Others have also joined publication on the celebration of the African American preaching tradition of which King and so many other sacred voices were a part.

Many slaves were exposed to a new religious system via Christianity. Many African systems of theology and worldview were strikingly different from the exposed biblical world. African slaves found that in Christianity there existed religious expression that was mostly in written form. This new religion was theologically classified in an entirely different motif than were the religious expressions on African soil. Albert Raboteau describes the encounter as one with a new exposure of faith. He asserts:

> . . . a fully articulated ritual relationship with the Supreme Being, who was pictured in the book the Christians called the Bible. Not just as Creator and Ruler of the Cosmos, but the God of History, a God who lifted up and cast down nations and peoples, a God where sovereign will was directing all things to an ultimate end, drawing good out of evil.[2]

With this cautious adaptation of the Christian God, slaves found a sense of spiritual energy in worship as related to their former religious culture. The idea of the African presence of spirit was later transposed into Christian expressions of immediacy. God, for them, was not a being that was very removed from human affairs, but, like the spirits, was a present and "right-now" God who executed justice for God's children. Much of the preaching to which slaves were exposed carried such tones of spiritual immediacy and power. This represented a certain type of "mystic presence" that was so often the center of praise and slave worship. The "God of the Bible" began to develop a lasting way of belief that merged with the gods of West Africa. It is important to note a few of the issues that assisted (encouraged) and issues that deterred (made difficult) the Africans' full acceptance of the Christian Bible.

Easy or encouraging factors were: 1. The Bible maintained a very clear "storytelling" nature that was open to the African griot;

2. Like many oral and ancient collections of stories, the Bible was revered as holy and sacred; 3. The Bible, as well as African folklore, is dominated by special characters and nationalistic themes (Israelites, etc.); 4. As was the spirit of Legba (West Africa's spirit of evil), themes of the spirit of Satan were grasped by slaves; and 5. In the desire for freedom and a new land of peace, "heaven" themes were very important teachings.

Difficult or biblical issues that were challenging to African traditional religious belief were: 1. Doctrines of salvation and developed, well-defined themes on the nature of the sacred; 2. Christianity's teachings regarding the "spirit" as a formal entity; 3. Office of the Trinity (as opposed to many divine beings and lesser divinities); 4. Doctrines of Original Sin; and 5. Confinement of God.

Scholars support the idea that strong, organized efforts to Christianize the slaves did not take place until the early 1700s. Thus, African religion and the spiritual importance of this religious "presence" were very vital in the lives and in the ongoing survival of the slave. This presence involved ongoing practices of many traditional African religious beliefs that centered upon everyday life, the spirits, ancestors, the gods, magic/medicine, and on the hereafter. Many of these theological issues were strongly embedded in the culture of everyday life experience. Praying, sacrificing, holy seasons, and fixed weekly ritual helped to inform the moral and social thought patterns in the African minds. The spiritual culture of indigenous Africa proved to be a vital source of life and reality testing for the African slave. African theologian John Mbiti reminds us of the strong character of African religion in culture:

> Religion . . . is by far the richest part of African heritage. It has dominated the thinking of African people to such an extent that it has shaped their cultures, their social life, the political organization, and economic activities. . . . Religion is so closely bound up with the traditional way of African life, while at the same time, this way has shaped religion.[3]

Traditional African religion, then, served as the basic life-defining source of direction for all of life. African slaves would continue to maintain religion as being an important source of survival, even in the new world. One could not understand the African without having an understanding of their spiritual world. This background included the role of higher divinities who maintained for them a careful guardianship of the universe and the physical elements therein, the many lesser divinities who gave personal attention to personal concerns, the overseeing and spiritual ancestors, and the elders with spiritual advice. Of course, the division of spirits into "recent dead" and "long dead" helped to explain the ongoing reliance upon these unseen protectors. Moreover, the trees, the rivers, the forests, and certain "ground" locations all became, for the African, a place of God's divine activity. It also bears noting that most West African slaves arrived here *with* the background of a religion where (like Christianity) one Creator God provided for the created, rules over the universe, is both mother and father spirit, and whose very nature is to have mercy and extend goodness.[4]

Visible, directed, and legally sanctioned worship space did not limit the expression of spirit and religious belief of the slave. As mentioned, the Invisible Institution was responsible for granting a sense of hope, esteem, and peace to the enslaved Africans. The worship gathering in this instance was often secret and gave way for open expressions, religious belief, and spiritual strength. In addition, this special worship with clandestine habitude often fed the pious imaginations of the slaves and gave definitions of justice and sacred equality. Among testimonies given by ex-slaves, certain themes remained constant regarding the Invisible Institution:

1. The importance of a private, divine space where freedom was experienced.
2. Ownership of a Christian belief system and code of religion that they could call their own.
3. The uncomplicated and less threatening manner of worship, conducted in the way of the folks, without outside interference.

4. The divinely inspired, minimally educated, but biblically articulate preachers, called from among the plantation folks.[5]

Thus, the religious imagination of the slaves was fed by their own idealization and duty of Christianity. African spirituality remained central in the expressions, the newly adopted theology of the Bible, and in various religious acts of the slave. Sociologist E. F. Frazier maintains that the slaves, through biblical Christianity, adopted a "new" sense of identity and communication. Further, he purports that there arose a new form of "social cohesion" as a result of Christian teaching.[6] Yet, much is to be desired from any conclusion that African sacred myth, religious practices, and theological insight were "exchanged" for Christianity. Perhaps the truth of the matter is that African religion became transposed along *with,* and not *instead of,* Christianity. Melva Costen makes another striking point:

> The symbolic presence of God in their midst harkens back to religious practices in Africa, where symbols of the presence of God were important. Another speculation is that an inverted pot is a representation of one of the symbols of the Yoruba god Esha Elegba. There are also ceremonies in the Caribbean where large vessels are used to hold water and sacred objects during religious ceremonies. Some of the slaves may have recalled this practice during the Middle Passage.[7]

The deeply spirited preaching of the gospel by slave preachers reflected this spiritual presence. They recalled African creator gods of spiritual justice and made connections with Christian insights. Henry Mitchell offers a very important historical observation:

> African traditional religion held that God is omnipotent (Olodumare of Yoruba) and omniscient (Brekyirihunugbe of the Ashanti). Couched in "praise names" such as these, traditional religion declared that the High God of bureaucratic monotheism is also just, and above all, provident.[8]

The preaching of the slave exhorter presented a spirited exercise in existential matters of survival. The Christian gospel was the main agenda. Yet, this holy agenda was also filled with insights of African religion, as well as a "different" reading of the biblical texts.

SPIRITUALS AS HERMENEUTICS

The *slave spiritual* served as a vital construct of the slave's interpretation of Christianity. Of course, these musical expressions of life, theodicy, hope, and moral concepts give us a lasting legacy of biblical interpretation on the part of these African bondspeople. In addition, this musical theology presented issues of God's justice, redemption ideals, judgment, and basic requirements of humans needed to remain in full divine/human fellowship. The very striking images of poetry bore witness that a more sovereign and merciful being was in full control of their destiny. This served to anchor their conviction that the institution of slavery would have an abrupt end. James Cone contends:

> The divine liberation of the oppressed from slavery is the central theological concept in the black spirituals. These songs show that black slaves did not believe that human servitude was reconcilable with their African past and their knowledge of the Christian gospel. They did not believe that God created Africans to be slaves of Americans. Accordingly, they sang of a God, who was involved in history—their history—making right what whites had made wrong.[9]

The spiritual was a form of musical theology that spoke to the heart of life's existence. As converts to Christianity, Africans held to native teachings, worldview, and cosmology. The lyrical musings of the songs were evidence to this fact. Identity was centered upon in the songs as well. As music was very holistic in the sacred culture, the hermeneutics of the spiritual reflected both the wedding of traditional African religion, as well as the formation of a separate system of biblical interpretation and celebration. This pre-academy theology reserved a heritage of religion that was founded on the premise that God is no "respecter" of persons. Among the major hermeneutical tasks of the spiritual are the following:

1. Expressions of courage and unity:
   "Walk together children, don't get weary . . ."
   "Run on, run on, keep your eyes on the prize . . ."
2. Citings of hypocrisy on the part of Christian teachers and missionaries:
   "Heaven, Heaven, everybody talking 'bout heaven ain't going there . . ."
   "Lord, I want to be a Christian in my heart . . ."
3. Double meanings of heaven as both otherworldly modifications, as well as freedom motifs on earth:
   "Follow the drinking gorge . . ."
   "Wade in the water, children . . ."
   "Let us break bread together . . ."
4. Loneliness and isolation:
   "Sometimes I feel like a motherless child . . ."
5. Protest to the slavery regime:
   "If I had my way, I'd tear this building down . . ."
   "God's gonna move this wicked race . . ."
6. Spirituals also, on occasion, pressed concerns of what David Goatley calls "Godforsakenness,"[10] or issues of theodicy.
7. Source of joy and peace:
   "Every time I feel the spirit . . ."

This tradition of musical hermeneutics was an important foundation of kerygmatic justice and hope. The preached word combined forces with oral traditions of African American theology to enhance and to elucidate the preached word.

As in colonial times, these songs of affirmation served as a basis for hope, unity, and courage during another turbulent era in our history—the Civil Rights struggle. During the King era, the spirituals continued to provide a source of life-changing hope and became a basis for important theo-political struggle and imagination. The spirituals were "transposed" into "Freedom Songs" by exchanging words and lines from traditional spirituals to reflect the situation and concerns of the present struggle. The familiar songs of protest and freedom were derived from existing spirituals that had been kept alive via oral tradition. This process, like the Invisible Institution, often called for group participation and spontaneous verse. For example, the Negro spiritual "I woke up this morning with my mind stayed on Jesus . . . " became "I woke up this morning with my mind stayed on freedom. . . . "

Or the song "This little light of mine, I'm gonna let it shine (3x). Let it shine (3x)" was amended in the 1950s to "All in the jailhouse, I'm gonna let it shine." Or,

> I want Jesus to walk with me
> I want Jesus to walk with me.
> All along this *pilgrim* journey. . . .

became:

> I want Jesus to walk with me
> I want Jesus to walk with me
> All along this *freedom* journey. . . .

Such lasting impressions were created and remained important for King's success in keeping connections to traditional spirituality and the challenging thrust for freedom. King, like the African griot, made much use of these oral traditions in his sermons. Other songs were essential in creating "topics" of unification for the masses ("Blowing in the Wind," for example). Perhaps the best example of an adaptation of a traditional spiritual/gospel song combination is "No More Auction Block for Me" and a gospel song written in 1900 by Charles Tinley entitled "I'll Overcome Some Day." Of course, this was transposed to a mainstay spiritual anthem and totem of the movement: "We Shall Overcome Some Day." (The similarities between spirituals, gospels, and freedom songs remained intact.)[11]

The slave preacher, then, worked much in the same mode as the singer of spirituals. Patterns of composites and steps of presentation were very analogous.

1. In composing a thought to share, the singer, as well as the preacher, improvised upon a song or sermon that already had been shared with the community. (This was very African and led to a new expression.)
2. The persons may have "combined" thoughts and images from existing ones.
3. There was the option of producing brand new thoughts for a song or sermon.[12]

The power of the spoken word, as well as the musically articulated word, provided much "bread" upon the waters of life for African American Christians.

Even with this unique and very directed hermeneutic of slave preaching, historians speculate that many black preachers took their messages to whites before they preached to their own counterparts. Slave preachers, trained and taught by Baptist and Methodist missionaries, were very often given sermonic privileges in these Eurocentric settings because of their "spiritual gifts." On the other hand, many colonial minds held that African slaves were pagan idol-worshipers who were void of a "soul." Thus, the summation was that the Christian gospel had no impact on such "savage minds." There was also much speculation that Christian baptism carried an evolving threat to status change. If a "fellow Christian" holds another "fellow Christian" as a bondsperson, a problematic issue arises in basic biblical doctrines of equality. As a result of this realization, the more pious slave owners were reluctant to change the stated conditions of bondage and did not extend excessive Christian baptism and evangelization to slaves.[13] In the absence of advance missionary activity before concentrated efforts of the Society for the Propagation of the Gospel (SPG) in 1701, slaves did indeed continue to call upon the gods of Africa. When the SPG opened avenues for Christian instruction, black worship was supervised to the utmost extent. There were, of course, no black separate congregations of worship in the South. The preacher admonished fellow slaves either during a "permitted" time of worship, or in the clandestine places of the Invisible Institution.

By the mid 1700s, many legendary slave preachers reached notoriety as a result of their abilities. Many graced the scenes of predominantly white pulpits. What was the major attraction and applicability of black slave preachers in an integrated setting? Mitchell suggests possible reasons:

1. Early in the slave experience, many masters required seven days of work instead of six . . . the denial of a day of rest was surely a factor in the lack of black gatherings where black preachers could be heard.
2. Preaching was not the most rewarding endeavor or respected calling in Colonial times, especially in the South. Hence, to speak to a white audience as a mere functionary under their control was one thing; but, to see one loose (with more freedom) among the slaves, saying what he really thought was another.
3. The black preachers offered not only a novelty, but also real talent and power. Thus, some whites . . . especially in new denominations already short of preachers . . . heard blacks gladly because they were the best preachers in a given location.[14]

DEVELOPMENT OF THE SLAVE PREACHING GENRE

As slaves exercised their spiritual culture and responded more fully to their needs of religious emotion, the art of preaching became a very central aspect of preserving African culture, as well as the day-to-day emotional and spiritual needs of the people. An Afro-Christian faith derived as a result of widespread acceptance and embracement of Christian teachings.

The preacher was very important in the maintenance and execution of this faith. He/she was central in the development of spiritual ideals and goals that created lasting effects on African American life and values. While the South remained predominantly loyal to baptism restrictions and cautions, the slaves' religious imagination was fostered by direct missionary activity during the colonial era. This missionary activity consisted of singing, praying, and teaching slaves to obey God's will, which generally was translated as being "good slaves." As mentioned, the antipode to the directed and missionary-led worship was the slaves' Invisible Institution, or Praise House meetings. In addition to the singing and praying "in the spirit," the preacher was a vital link in directing encouragement and creative spiritual release. Charles Joyner commented on the slave preachers' importance. He stated:

> Utilizing ritualized language and behavior as symbolic action, they [preachers] transformed religious ritual through transcendental ecstasy into structured meaning, renewing and recycling the energies of the slave community. They often mediated between the slaves' Christian beliefs and the workday world of the low country.[15]

The spiritual task of the black slave preacher was to "correct" those "lies" of the gospel that had been pressed upon the masses by white preachers in missionary slave churches. This included justification of slavery and black inferiority and glorifications of God's "pleasure" with the institution of bondage. In addition, it was necessary to redirect catechism lessons that often distorted the traditional kerygma of the biblical text in favor of distortions that supported the slavery regime. Dwight Hopkins notes this catechism example:

> Q. When Abraham took his 318 slaves, and pursued the kings, why did they not run away as slaves do now?

> A. Either because Abraham had his hounds along, or because God had taught them better.[16]

It was a survival necessity for black slave preachers to undo the damages and powers of evil that lurked in these characters of "the demonic in the Scripture and theological doctrine with exclusive benefits for the owner."[17] Fellow slaves relied upon the preacher's words and unique style of delivery and interpretation to also foster a sense of community, social order, role model, and ritual. Hence, slave preachers served a very crucial function.

The fear of African American religious expression was not as great in the North. The opportunity for preaching and religious activity was not as guarded as was the southern ideal. Instead of the many "secret" worship communities of the southern plantations, the early North afforded a few more institutionalized church settings for blacks. The earliest record of a group of blacks organizing for a religious meeting occurred in Massachusetts under the leadership of a Puritan cleric by the name of Cotton Mather. Mather drew up a set of *Rules for Society of Negroes*, suggesting ordered conduct and compliance to Fugitive Laws. He later wrote the celebrated treatise, *The Negro Christianized*, which encouraged concern and renewed activity on the part of the SPG.[18] Such support and evangelization activity in this area of the colonies helped to increase the number of black preachers, both slave and free.

As a result of the visibility of black itinerant preachers, the forces of Afro-Christian religious values were institutionalized in the life and culture of the people. The preacher represented a sense of African spirituality that was connected to new definitions of life and humanity. Realms of spiritual power were realized that became foundations for a different, but essential, definition of the cosmos. From the very sophisticated preaching and theological presentation of Lemuel Hayes in the Congregational tradition, to the emotional soul-searching depth of Black Harry, to the challenged, but spirited, expressions of Jarena Lee, the black preaching style was a major aspect of theology, spirituality, and social expression. As a matter of fact, African American theology was dispersed to a non-academy style by the slave preacher long before the term became a mainstay. Whites described this form of preaching as "sonorous," meaning tonal, and there is much evidence to show that the voice variations were very spirited with sincerity and founded upon African influence.[19]

Richard Allen, Absalom Jones, David George, George Liele, and many others left legacies of both preaching and leadership as they challenged the roots of racist evangelical theology and established separate worship space for blacks. These independent "Freedom Churches" prevail today as a sacred monument to justice hermeneutics and to the worship of a liberating God.

HYMNS AND PREACHING

Along with preaching, Afro-Baptist and Afro-Methodist traditions of hymn-lining enhanced the musical genre that was available to the preacher. In addition to the spirituals, slaves were soon exposed to the singing of hymns or "psalms." Worship attendance and the Revival movements of the late 1700s and early 1800s brought new religious fervor as a result of much "revived" preaching and singing. For example, during the Great Awakening of 1730, a lively tone of worship was the style for all. Colonists and missionaries found that four-five stanza hymns were more spiritual than chants. John and Charles Wesley, John Newton, Richard Allen, and others soon contributed to a repertoire of musical hermeneutics. This would especially prove to be an enhancement for black preachers in that, like their sermons, the songs usually told a story of salvation or eschatology:

> Amazing grace how sweet the sound
> That saved a wretch like me.
> I once was lost, but now am found
> Was blind, but now I see.[20]

New biblical insights on justice would also arise from the lyrics of these gospel hymns of the 1800s. The African American worshiping community developed into a strong center for racial support and awareness as Jim Crow laws forced them to sanctify their identity.

As we continue to discuss the legacy of African American preaching, we come to a very important issue as it relates to the continued development and phenomenon of the spoken word. There are two important interrogations raised by Mitchell that relate to the effectiveness of Martin Luther King Jr. and many other African American preachers:

> As one ponders the rapid growth of the early black church and the other evidence of the effective leadership of the early black preachers, two significant questions arise: (1) What was their preaching like? and (2) Where did they get their style or tradition?[21]

CHAPTER TWO

ATTRIBUTES OF THE VOCAL "BREAD OF HEAVEN"

African American Sermonic Peculiarities

NARRATIVE/STORY APPROACH

MOST THEOLOGIANS OF HERMENEUTICS find that the narrative is among the most common homiletical expressions of the preaching tradition. Especially in the African American preaching genre, the narrative (sermon) has held much importance in the religious culture. The story as told in a narrative and descriptive form becomes very engaging. James Evans suggests this description:

> If the form of black religion is the story, then the form of black theology must be narrative. The two aspects of black religion, the praxeological and the hermeneutical, can be held together only by a form of discourse that reconciles the two types of activity— praxis and criticism—that have been separated by Enlightenment thought.[1]

The suggestion here is that the oral form of theological discourse is of primary importance in the religious culture of African Americans. In addition to stirring (biblical) exegesis of biblical texts, the story also carries moral and political impetus. The early preaching of African Americans placed God in the very center of their sacred imagination. As the message unfolded, the focal point pressed upon the activity of a just God who managed the affairs of the world with a just righteousness. Olin Moyd makes a connection between the spiritual implications and the justice implications found in traditional sermonic oral narrative:

> God's attributes are summed up in the oral folk sermons—not in puzzling, esoteric, or mystical terms such as "omnipotent," "omniscient," and "omnipresent," but as "so high you can't get over him, so wide you can't get around him (God), and so low that you can't get under him." This practical theology is a theology of affirmation rather than a theology of explanation. This practical theology provides biblical and divine answers to the questions raised [in] . . . an unjust society.[2]

In most cases, the story developed formulation with an imaginative ideal of injustice that was weakened as the power of "right" prevailed. Favorite dominant themes of sermonic expression come to mind such as: "Daniel in the Lion's Den," "Moses at the Red Sea," "Shadrach, Meshach, and Abednego," and "Elijah and the Prophets of Baal," to name a few.

Narrative preaching in the African American religious tradition is very intent on *sermon shape*.[3] This effective use of preaching art employs the juxtaposition of conflicted ideals, national/discussive argument, metaphorical inquiry, and the use of extended illustration. The essence of sermonic shape is found in the preacher's ability to "tell the story" with loyalty to these issues. This form of homiletics, also known as *story preaching*,[4] is yet a mainstay in African American pulpits. Other technical names for this form include *episodal preaching* and *inductive preaching*.[5] Inductive preaching comports the use of deduction of thought and adroit movements of ideas from a simplistic approach to one that is more particular. Episodal preaching makes use of a connected sequence of events that generally find a common unity either *during* the progression or *at the conclusion* of the spiritual dialogue. References to "good gospel preaching" are filled with examples whereby the preacher is excitedly engaged in demonstrating the truths of his/her message with the skillful and spirited use of deduction and episode. Note this dynamic episodal ending to a challenging sermon by Carolyn Ann Knight:

> Jesus made a name for himself. At that name, demons tremble, governments topple, blind folks can see, lame folks can walk, deaf folks can hear. At that name the dead shall live again. At that name every knee shall bow and every tongue shall confess that he is Lord to the glory of God.
>
> Jesus Christ says to you and to me: If thou be a great people, stand up, get up into the hill country . . . live your life. Realize your dreams. Let your light shine. Blow your trumpet. Sing your song. . . .[6]

BIBLICAL NARRATION IN AFRICAN AMERICAN PREACHING

Good narrative preaching in this folk tradition is also character-ized by a concentrated and authoritative use of the Bible. The Bible has held crucial significance as the critical, as well as celebrated, moral guide within the culture. From slave preachers to the cur-rent innovative preachers of today, a great skill of the narrative is found in an effective use of scripture. Historically, the Bible has served African American culture as a means of communication, survival, and hope. Hence, these truths that rest upon the pages of the sacred canon are quite life-defining. The articulation and in-terpretation of the same have been manifested with skill and care. Vincent Wimbush offers a very important fact regarding this im-portance of biblical interpretation:

> One useful way of beginning to clarify the issues involved in thinking about the function of the Bible among African Americans is to think of the Bible as a language, even language world. . . . A great many of the slaves did adopt . . . as part of the complex phenomenon of acquiring a number of new skills, symbols, and languages for survival . . . the Bible as a "language" through which they negotiated both the strange new world called America and the slave existence.[7]

With this historical veracity, it is easy to understand the nature of good biblical narration as a vital aspect of folk preaching. Imagination (explained later in this discussion), folk belief, and spirituality are energized and fused in a unique manner as the story is told and retold directly from God's Word. Scriptural testimonials of a just and fair God who always triumphed over evil folks have carried very special meaning in this religious tradition. Such biblical "language" has resulted in many lessons of hope, survival, and eschatology via the hermeneutics that are based on the conceptions of the God of the Bible. Sermonic biblical narration served to uplift sober images of the Creator's power over malevolent and wicked enemies, and even of God's victory over nature. Over the years, this talent of spiritual interpretation has fed the imagination of hope and determination for many.

The reality of everyday life is often closely connected with the pathos of biblical characters who are portrayed in the unwinding story of human salvation and divine grace. Those promises of redemption, presence, and inner virtue are paramount in the sociohistorical fibers and in the general *sitz en laben* of the people. The preacher, with such language, echoes that the relationship of God's ongoing activity in this imperfect cosmos is still very important. Thus, the biblical narrative yields much "dynamism." People seek a weekly spiritual reminder that the Pharaohs, the Nebuchadnezzars, the Belshazzars, or even the Pilates of this world do not have the final verdict. I agree with Henry Mitchell on the suggestion of a unification of "story" and "teller" when it comes to executing the text:

As true of all good storytelling, the Black Bible story must first be a good work of art in its own right. The teller must tell as if the telling were an end in itself, though it might at times be felt that there must be interspace asides. These point out the relevance of the story's action, which might be missed. At all times, while the story is being told, the teller is caught up in it as if it had been witnessed personally.[8]

Congregations are often riveted to the narrative as if by hanging on to each word. The biblical story is *their* story. It is a story that translates a unique theology. The preacher has a special appreciation for the story. (We will later demonstrate King's use of the biblical narrative.) Without the biblical narrative, the sermon may have a mere "lecture" possibility. Wyatt T. Walker also presses this point regarding "The Book":

> Black preaching has always had a quality of deep Biblicalism. Authentic preaching in the folk tradition comes from the Bible. Now, I know who Deitrich Bonhoffer is, and Paul Tillich and the Barthian theologians on the continent. . . . The central focus of my preaching is Jesus Christ, crucified, dead, buried, and risen on the third day morning. . . . The emphasis is on *The Book* because the people know *The Book*. Their view is from the inside out. The people are in *The Book*.[9]

The narrative of life and of life's expectations is central in the preached word. There is little wonder that the sermon remains the most important facet of African American Christian worship. The narrative form is still a very popular approach to the gospel.

THE ROLE OF IMAGINATION IN THE SACRED ORAL TRADITION

Imagination provides much effect to the narrative sermon. While the narrative sermon takes us upon a spiritual route with a directed and very intentional end, it is the skilled use of imagination that keeps the material "alive" and interesting. Of course, any biblical hermeneutic that is reflective of the variance of black preaching is not confined to one form of preaching genre. In other words, in addition to narrative, other forms of scriptural genre that reflect the mighty acts of a loving God are important as well. This includes the genre of proverb, psalm, epistle, parable, and narrative.[10] The point, then, is that imagination helps to shape the intended message by the use of any scriptural form. Historically, African American clergy have not always enjoyed the fine gifts of literacy and academic theological training. In many cases, the gift of spiritual imagination accented sermonic presentation with realistic interpretations and applications. The gifts of producing vivid and powerful images of the sacred kerygma left lasting impressions and memory. Thomas Troeger defines this notion as "imagination theology":

> Imaginative theology employs visionary and integrative capacities of the mind to create theological understanding. It uses power of observation to become receptive to the Holy Spirit, who works upon our consciousness thought patterns of association and juxtaposition. . . . [It] utilizes those patterns to evoke similar reflections in the listeners.[11]

In this case, imagination refers to a sense of color, power, and spirit that connects with the existing authority of the Word. Folk preaching traditions have held this phenomenon in high importance. Spoken practical theology is indeed a product of those given life-based domains of existence that call for a careful imaginative observation. James Cone finds agreement:

> Theology is . . . human speech informed by historical and theological traditions, and written for particular times and places. Theology is contextual language . . . that is defined by the human situation that gives birth to it.[12]

The contextual language of traditional preaching has maintained these implications of spiritual imagination. When the preacher spiritually positions him/herself to feel the Word, a subsequent interpretive theology follows that is characterized by a depth of spiritual and imaginative musings. It is this point of reference that inspires many preachers in witness of this gift to often retort: "In my mind's eye . . . " or "I would imagine. . . . "[13] The operative advantage of this mental eye allows the preacher to help persons foresee possibilities of moving beyond pain and agony to aspirations of peace and tranquil hope.

In many cases, it is the flowing, poetic, picturesque biblical imaginings that place the hearer directly in that sun-drenched, lonesome, dark valley of bones with Ezekiel, or even by the cross, beholding the lunar eclipse and listening to the last painful mortal words of the Savior. Poetic imagination is a traditional gift in black preaching. The poetical nature of the homily generally gives way to a sure and sound truth of the faith. William McClain cites an example of this preached poetry in an excerpt from a sermon given by the famous Baptist leader, Dr. J. H. Jackson of the National Baptist Convention:

> But I say to you my friends, fear not tomorrow, and shine not from the task or the lot that is yet to come. The future belongs to God, and the last chapter in this human life will not be written by the blood-stained hands of godless men, but by the God of history. The same hand that raised the curtain of creation and pushed both the floating worlds upon the broad sea of time and flashed forth the light of life that put an end to ancient chaos and darkness . . . erected the highways of the skies and rolled the sun like a golden ball across the pavement of the dawn. . . .[14]

Again, this aspect of theological poetry has indeed been a most powerful medium of hermeneutics in the African American religious folk tradition. African spirits of holism and sacred expressions of completeness of sacred unity are reflected in the summations of God's presence and actions as interpreted via preaching. Intentionality is employed in keeping the vocal Word "alive" and understandable. It is in this vein that preachers subscribe to the theory as suggested by the early church father Origen, that the Word has a significant sense of imagination when the scriptural text employs a threefold sense of existence: the existence of a flesh, the existence of a soul or moral nature to awaken the human soul to a holy life, and the existence of spirit or mystic sense that results in union with God.[15]

Hence, the use of sacred poetry results in a flowing and very involving theology that leaves a very clear and precise interpretation. When "flesh" is established in the narrative, the sermon assumes a "soul" as witness to authenticate the sacred claims. Finally, the moving and centered spirit "arrives" to foster a deep sense of commitment and acceptance of the Word. Imagination and poetry serve as co-producers of spirited worship. (Subsequent chapters will note this effective use of poetry and theological imagination in the voice of Martin Luther King Jr.)

INVOLVEMENT AND REPETITION

Participant *involvement* is an enduring trait that is found in traditional African American preaching. The speaker and the hearer make contact that encourages an action of rapport. As opposed to those traditions that consist of a careful homily that is presented in quiet and attentive reception, a very deliberate spirit of dialogue occurs. This dialogue consists of verbal communications and spontaneous reactions of oral response by congregants to signal a unified reception of the message in process. In many cases, this form of oral communication is anticipated by the preacher and it often serves as a temperance of his/her effectiveness (or noneffectiveness) of interpretation. The preaching act is an "involving" reminder of God's movement and action in the world. Of course, the heart of African American folk religion centers upon a god who "acts." As a reminder of the central preaching hermeneutic of experience, Moyd finds that the "power of God is not theory. The power of God is action."[16] Since God's power is seen as an *activity*, the community looks forward to the experience of being a dynamic entity of the same. Involvement in the African American preaching tradition creates a unified spiritual ground of truth for all. The experience of preaching the "whole counsel" has always rested upon this unified effort to find a common ground of witness and experience. Melva Costen suggests the power that derives from this experience:

> An important characteristic of hermeneutics in black preaching is the empowerment of the preacher to create an atmosphere wherein the preacher and listener might hear the Word by *experiencing* it. The preacher must be so familiar with the story that he/she during the preaching moment *becomes* the Biblical character ... the test is internalized so that it is transferred, and comes alive to the context of the preacher. The goal is to create an atmosphere in which the listeners can themselves become the Word of God incarnate at that moment.[17]

The form of spiritual empowerment via involvement is reflected in the deliberate antiphonal quality and patterns of direct participation by given congregations. While this form is not new to the African American tradition, theologian Fred Craddock introduced a related style of preaching in the 1970s known as *inductive preaching*. This approach was a challenge to traditional Eurocentric deductive preaching and called for more participation on the part of the hearers:

> The inductive method begins with the particulars of human experience and moves toward the often surprising conclusions of the Gospel ... the preacher enables the congregation to participate actively in the movement and meaning of the sermon.[18]

Involvement cultivates a sense of full communion and makes for the proverbial "one accord" in worship. Scholars from W. E. B. Dubois to Diana Hayes have studied and marveled at this cultural attribute of spirituality. Some, such as Evans Crawford, suggest that this moment is so alluring that there is an ordered scale of witness and response:

1. "Help 'em Lord" (moments of prayerful attention).
2. "Well?" (contemplation).
3. "That's all right!" (witness to truth).
4. "Amen!" (acknowledgment that the preacher is on the same wavelength).
5. "Glory Hallelujah!" (spiritual pinnacle).[19]

In each of these movements, the response is significant. Such communication (or lack thereof) does signify much regarding the common realm that is sought. It is interesting to note that many traditional clergy held to a practice of calling upon motionless objects to bear witness to musings that may have been less popular or glorious, but were instructive. ("Say Amen, lights; say Hallelujah, windows," etc.) At any rate, the involvement was always celebrative because *God* was focus and center. The anticipation of rehearsing the good news of God's presence and action did also warrant response and witness. The hermeneutics of traditional African American preaching maintained a distinct authority, simply because it remained focused, not on a philosophical statement of life, but on God. On this issue, I agree wholeheartedly with Cleophus LaRue in his summation of the critical significance of God talk in the African American sermon:

> The preacher who would preach with a certain sense of authority and accomplishment in the tradition of the black church must always remember that at its heart the black sermon is about God. . . . The most effective preaching is preaching that conveys with clarity and insight how God acts in concrete situations in the lives of those who hear the gospel. . . . [20]

Hearing creative truths regarding God's existence and unfailing providence in the cosmos always bears a sense of "witnessing" involvement.

Complementing this form of antiphony is the direct use of *repetition*. This form of sacred verbalization is akin to African styles of chant and ritual. Various lines, themes, or points are intentionally repeated in an effort to produce an accentuation upon the given subject or illustration. This effect, when actualized, carries much potential for unified involvement and concentration. As a result, the audience has a tendency to respond in antiphony. Each time a spiritual stress is made to press a particular issue, a "melody-like" response ensues. For example, note a familiar sermonic call-and-response antiphony that is based on a repetitive interpretation of Matthew 11:2–6, where Jesus sends a report to an inquisitive and imprisoned John the Baptist who, through his (John's) disciples, is queried regarding Jesus' messiahship:

Am I the expected one, he asks? I want you to go back and tell John a few things. You bear witness and tell John what you have seen. Go back and tell him that everything is under control—

Go tell John that formerly blind folk can now see the beautiful sun rise—

Go tell John that the former lame folk no longer lay on pallets of misery; but now go running through the city, telling what God has done—

Go tell John that the hungry are now fed the Gospel bread and are full with new vision—

Tell John that the thirsty have found the Living Water and a spring of flowing peace—

Go back and tell John that weeping may endure for a night, but joy will come in the morning!—

Find John and tell him to hold on, everything will be all right—

Most of all, tell John that I have it all under control and that whoever believes in me has eternity—

One notes that here the sentence structure is very deliberate as to enhance the effectiveness of the textual background. These clergy of the tradition who are considered "masters" of the pulpit are those who are skilled in effective repetition. (Again, I note *effective* repetition.) The repeated action of refrain invites the listener to become involved in a supportive and responsive manner as the chorus echoes the repeated line.

RHYTHM/SERMONIC MUSICAL NATURE

A closely related phenomenon of the former discussion is that of *rhythm* and the musical nature of folk preaching. The two items are mentioned together because of their similar qualities. Musical nature and rhythmic aspects are analogies to repetition in many ways; but, also, there are definitive distinctions between the two.

It is important to remember that African religion was "danced" religion and not just a stationary worship. The ritual nature of African religion is characterized by consistent movement during worship. Hence, as slaves practiced Christian worship, movement and dance remained consequential as religious expression. It would follow that since most forms of Afro-Christianity were oral in nature, the preached, as well as the sung theology, bore impending qualities of rhythm. Just as the priest and the juju man on the mother sail, the African American preacher made use of an unparalleled combination of chant, rhythm, and vocal variations. Legendary preachers such as Black Harry, Shubal Sterns, and Daniel Marshall of the colonial period began to set the pace for the impending "holy whine" tonality for years to come.[21]

It is important to note that the chanted sermon was also a tradition of white missionary preachers during the Great Awakening era when sermons were presented with great emotion. Nevertheless, this style has remained an archetype that was also reflected in African American spirituals, gospel songs, blues, and folk tales. Given the very oral nature of the culture, this style of preaching prevailed throughout history and provided a sense of "wisdom, information, advice, and not least, sheer enjoyment for generations of African Americans."[22]

One cannot deny the fact that the very rhythmic elements of African speech and music are contributing to the "melody" of traditional African American preaching. The sounds, the beats, the pentatonic nature of delivery and the lingering "hum" of the excited sentences encourage participation. Let us consider this retrospective:

> While the congregation is participating in the sermonic event and gets involved in the rhythm of the preaching, the verbal response coming from the congregation increasingly falls within the intervals where the preacher metrically pauses to take a breath. This call and response . . . is a crucial texture found wherever traditional black oratory occurs.[23]

Liturgical intonations occur as the spirit brings these two elements together. It is very common to observe a sing-song quality as the message progresses. In the tradition, this has been referred to as "whooping." In a study of African speech and hymnody, Walter Pitts relates this tradition of preaching to culture:

> One of the most striking features that distinguishes Afro-American preaching from Euro-American preaching styles is the chanted quality of the black sermon. . . . [The] sermon and prayer may become so melodious as they develop that church musicians can easily accompany the preacher's and deacon's patterns of intonation on their instruments. Piano and organ can become involved in a melodic antiphony like that of the congregation echoing the melody of the sermons and prayers as they evolve.[24]

Since vocal quality becomes very important in many worshiping communities, the tendency at many times to whoop may arrive at a premature moment. The level of spirit and participation by the congregation may encourage the preacher to move on to higher meter and to often search for more "power" to allow the dialogue to continue. However, there is a warning that this type of movement be done with caution and "responsibility" of the spirit. Henry Mitchell explains:

> Dynamite has to be handled carefully and applied to tasks stringently selected. If God is to bless a less inhibited communication of the gospel, the preacher must be especially careful not to succumb to the temptation to let emotional momentum carry him or her beyond that which is mandated by the Holy Spirit.[25]

What Mitchell alludes to is the fact that one must not be driven by a *personal* mandate to force spirit if the authentic binding of God is not there. Nor should one feel so inclined to present a "false" presentation of the Word that is to satisfy a personal agenda. In the next chapter, we will discuss the careful movements of Martin Luther King Jr. in this regard. He was a "mover" of the spirits of people. However, he was certain that his content was responsible and that his approach was in concert with a responsible message. In sermonic delivery, the warning is not to "peer toward the mountain" before it is time to "leave the valley." Many a preacher have made this common misjudgment.

Nevertheless, the musical nature of these call-and-response patterns is very important in the history and preservation of African American preaching. King was very skilled in his type of musical oratory. As later sections will demonstrate, his nature of speaking was marked by a certain rhythm that carried a very responsible and directed truth.

SILENCE AND PAUSE

While the call-and-response form of preaching is very widespread in the tradition, it is important to note that *pause* and *silence* are also effective instruments of homiletical genius. There are so many times that the sermon is very powerful as a "quiet adagio movement that gradually builds to scherzo celebration or a sonata allegro form with numerous recapitulations and a lengthy coda."[26] The drama of the sermon is oftentimes accented by a quiet approach or a pause movement that forces a sense of awareness and attention. Symbolized in such great mystic preachers as Howard Thurman, the dramatic pause makes connection with the spirit and audience as very intentional and directed meditation is encouraged by this technique. A great master of style, Thurman was gifted in the use of the "thought" process in the preaching dynamic. Crawford recalls:

> Nobody made use of the pause like Howard Thurman. Students who have traveled hundreds of miles to hear him speak, have been known to call him great just for [his] rising, standing at the pulpit or podium, rubbing his hand over his face, and looking skyward before uttering his first word. His pauses initially seemed to embody what speakers call the "dramatic pause." . . . The spells of silence related to his speaking are related to meditation and are best called "meditative pauses" given what went before and after them.[27]

Preachers such as Thurman were able to use this effect to create a spiritual atmosphere whereby a unity of worship would take place. By employing the pause and the occasional silence, the listener is forced to stay on the same wavelength and to meditate in crescendo: "He went down into the pit. [pause] I wonder why. [long pause] [renewed vigor] To save our souls and snatch us from eternal danger!" When we hear preachers such as Thurman, Martin Luther King Jr., or M. C. Williams, we find a strong appreciation for the "powerful silence" in the spoken word. This is a very important alternative to the established and often blaring "whooping" presentation that is so well appreciated. Historic, cultural, great pulpiteers such as Lemmuel Hayes and Gardner Taylor did not employ this very boisterous spiritual presence. Nevertheless, their mild-mannered but theologically powerful sermonic style is celebrated as unique.

CHAPTER THREE

CUTTING FROM THE "SAME LOAF"

King and African American Preaching

MARTIN LUTHER KING JR. AS A PARADIGM OF THE SLAVE PREACHER

Saga of Slave Experience

MUCH OF MARTIN LUTHER KING JR.'s oral theology was a rehearsal of the historic yearnings for freedom of African Americans during the slave experience in this country. The enslavement motif was often a major source of his dialogues regarding a continued drive for human equality during the twentieth century. With a strong appreciation of history and the struggle for justice in this country, he often alluded to the strength and determination of our mothers and fathers during this time. He always called upon the nation to review history and to come to a realization that a sense of "moral" slavery was still in existence. In an address, King made this observation:

> It is time that we stopped our blithe lip service to the guarantees
> of life, liberty, and pursuit of happiness. These fine sentiments are
> embodied in the Declaration of Independence, but that document
> was always a declaration of intent rather than of reality. There were
> slaves when it was adopted, and, to this day, black Americans have
> not life, liberty, nor the privilege of pursuing happiness. . . . [1]

Expressions of Slave Theology and Experience in King's Preaching

As the slave preacher sought to present a gospel of encouragement and one of determination, the words of King were filled with admonitions of the same. He was filled with a sense of prophetic theology that always raised questions of the ordered manner of injustice. In the tradition of the slave preacher, King found comfort in using unique oral skills to interpret a special gospel of existence. Keith Miller makes this observation:

> Ignoring print culture, folk preachers nurtured and polished their high oral form of religious art, which they perfected despite the harshness of slavery. White observers often noted the awesome oratorical skills of popular slave preachers. Electrifying sermons ensured not only the propagation of Christianity but possibly the continued existence of African American people.[2]

The preacher was critical in defining the cosmic order as well as the spiritual order of the universe. With a strong interpretative spirit, the preacher also fostered a sense of hope for existence by very moving examples and explications of the nature of God, even in the midst of an unjust system.

King often referred to the slavery experience to give impetus to the freedom struggle. Moreover, like the slave preacher, his unique oral talent helped to give encouragement for ongoing hope, identity, and strength. On occasion, his sermons were filled with very striking references to the slavery experience. In "A Knock at Midnight," he speaks of a spiritual sense of "midnight desperation" and makes example of the slavery experience:

> Our eternal message of hope is that dawn will come. Our slave foreparents realized this. They were never unmindful of the fact of midnight, for always there was the rawhide whip of the overseer and the auction block where families were torn asunder to remind them of its reality. When they thought of the agonizing darkness

of midnight, they sang:

Oh, nobody knows de trouble I've seen,
    Glory Hallelujah!
. . . Encompassed by a staggering midnight but believing that
morning would come, they sang:
I'm so glad trouble don't last always.
O my Lord, O my Lord, What shall I do?[3]

He often used this motif to point to the fact that there was a
different kind of slavery. A slavery of injustice and hatred was the
order of the day. Therefore, the theology of this folk-type preacher
was always seeking to make a difference in the salvation expectation of the people. While many slave preachers expounded on
otherworldly values and the afterlife, King's expositions on the
"other world" consisted of a unified realm of dwelling where peace
and harmony could exist in this world. As we will note in the biblical discussion, there was much use of Old Testament figures and
images. This was very much in the tradition of slave religion as
well. These were figures who had reached a sense of victory and
triumph over evil foes. There were many "foes" of justice and many
"Pharaohs" who did not want to see God's children live in freedom. This was a central theme of King's hermeneutics. Many of
his sermons bore effective quotes from slavery spirituals. Of his
favorites were:

1. Free at Last
2. Balm in Gilead
3. Climbing Jacob's Ladder
4. Swing Low
5. Before I Be a Slave
6. Bye and Bye I'm Gonna Lay Down My Heavy Load
7. All God's Chillun Got Wings[4]

A sense of hope and powerful stirring for freedom was fostered
by King's understanding of the unfinished democracy that was

dug by our founding fathers, as well as by our slavery mothers and fathers. It was the African American religious experience that helped to shape the future of the ideals of justice and the implementations for freedom. Lewis Baldwin observes:

> King's idea of freedom and justice was also rooted in a faith, a hope, and an activism that developed out of the black religious experience . . . if Lawrence Jones is right in saying that the slaves dreamed of and struggled for a community where freedom, justice, and equality guaranteed by the Constitution and Declaration of Independence would prevail, then it was Martin Luther King's vision of the evolved Community that the greatest heritage of their ideas is to be found. In other words, in their struggle against slavery, black people have made a significant contribution by providing a prophetic vision of freedom, justice, and equality . . . through the life and work of King.[5]

This spiritual influence of King upon the masses was often the result of his appreciation of the slave preacher and the knowledge of the slave preacher's unique gift and responsibility. King, like the slave preacher, gave the people "something on the inside" to stand up for amid the difficulties of their days. There was a particular ability of articulation within the varied gifts of the leader that pressed his ability to articulate their dreams and hopes as well. King was very much in touch with the pain, the fear, the hopes, and the dreams of his people; hence, his sermonic ability was grounded in a deep compassion and concern. Citing the spiritual presence of the slave preacher, King described the preacher in this manner:

> He didn't know much about Plato or Aristotle. He never would have understood Einstein's theory of relativity if Einstein had been in existence at that time. But he knew God. And he knew that the God that he had heard about, and read about, was not a God that would subject some of his children and exalt the others. And he

would get there with his broken language. He didn't know how to make his subject and verb agree, you know. He didn't have that. But he knew somehow that there was an agreement with an eternal power.[6]

In many of his actions, experiences, and theological development, King found that the slave preacher was a very significant entity in the development of the African American oral religious tradition as well as a very important trailblazer for the quest of freedom and equality. Moreover, the saga of slavery and the experience of captivity were major directives and starting points for the leader to bring a sense of reality to many concerns of justice that remained unchanged. In his most famous address, "I Have a Dream," King called attention to this assertion:

Five score years ago, a great American, in whose symbolic shadow we stand today, signed the Emancipation Proclamation. This momentous decree came as a great beacon and light of hope to millions of Negro slaves who had been seared in the flames of withering injustice. It came as a joyous daybreak to end the long night of their captivity. But one hundred years later, the Negro still is not free; one hundred years later, the life of the Negro is still sadly crippled by the manacles of segregation and the chains of discrimination. . . . [7]

Thus, many of the images, concerns, and theology found in King's preaching would be the result of his understanding and consciousness of this "unfinished business" of justice.

KING'S USE OF THE NARRATIVE FORM

Storytelling Skills

As a great storyteller in the tradition of African American preaching, King was considered a master of the narrative preaching style. We previously discussed various references to this style and preaching form (episodal preaching, story preaching, inductive preaching). Such forms and modes highlight the effectiveness of story form in the preaching event. An interesting additional example to this grouping is a category to which John Killinger makes reference known as "the faceting sermon."[8] It is explained in this manner:

> Faceting is what jewelers do to precious stones after the stones have been split; they cut faces on the stones so that their beauty may be more easily seen. . . . [As] the jeweler cuts and polishes, dimensions of the beauty begin to leap out of prison. . . . It is the same with the faceting sermon. The preacher begins by splitting open some great truth . . . then the preacher sets to work around that trait, polishing side effects until the whole sermon sparkles.[9]

King could begin a sermon that dealt with a very crucial concern and could shape and "shine" the truth of God's promise or presence. By the time he reached the end of the sermon, it sparkled with destiny. He could develop a particular issue and remain very focused on the subject matter. With his very skillful oratory, he held intently one's attention until he finally reached the "punch" of the narrative. In the tradition of the African griot, the slave preacher, and the tradition of the early twentieth century black preacher, King was a marksman at using his vocal talent and combined it with his fine learning and religious experience. This presented a great narrative form. In the sermon "The Answer to a Perplexing Question," note the skillful progression of narrative:

1. The text based on Matthew 17:19 is introduced and followed by a perplexing question concerning the eradication of evil in the universe on the part of humans:

> Human life through the centuries has been characterized by man's persistent efforts to remove evil from the earth . . . the problem that has hampered man has been his inability to conquer evil.[10]

Having raised the issue of contemplation, he then goes on to inductively press the issue of evil and the nature of an evil society.

It is important to note that inclusive language had not been a major mode of communication during King's legacy. Most of his writings, as prolific as they are, were usually in the masculine gender.

2. In two separate sections, he deductively concentrates on two spurious propositions on the human expectation of casting out evil: 1) removal of evil by means of humanity's own power and self-directed resolution, and 2) removal of expectations by means of an anticipated divine eschatological purging.

3. In both discussions, he keeps such an intricate issue alive by presenting interesting real life concerns combined with striking historical and biblical images, and moral insights. For example:

> Does all of this reveal the fallacy of thinking that God will cast evil from the earth, even if man does nothing except to sit complacently by the wayside? No prodigious thunderbolt will blast away evil. No mighty army of angels will descend. . . . Always [humanity] must do something.[11]

4. In a surprise move, after one awaits and holds on to each uttered statement about this perplexing question of removing evil, he suggests an awaited resolve:

> The answer is found in an idea which is distinctly different from the two we have discussed. . . . Evil can be cast out, not by man alone nor by a dictatorial God who invades our lives, but when we open the door and invite God through Christ to enter.[12]

The story form of the old African American church was always a method of King's approach. He carefully arranged and plotted his thoughts and points. There was generally a directed beginning, but the sermon would often journey with poems, historical data, spirituals, and illustrations. This, as a distinct character of the narrative sermon, preempted a "strategic delay of the preacher's message."[13] A great example of this style is a message entitled "Facing the Challenge of a New Age," delivered in 1956 to the First Annual Institute on Non-Violence and Social Change. As he addressed the gathering, King was proposing that a new era of social change was about to emerge. The audience was taken on a breathtaking journey of history and moral questioning. Their minds were focused on an exciting blend of statistics; racial concerns; biblical injunctions; the poetry of William Shakespeare, William Mallock, James Russell Lowell, and John Hollander; and Christocentric directives. The conditions of the "new age" were unfolded as he poetically cited the need for supportive integration, moral courage, and boldness in justice. His strategy in this long but interesting narrative form was to lead to a vision of hope and unity for such a new age:

> If we will join together in doing all of these things, we will be able to speed up the coming of the new world—a new world in which men will live together as brothers [and] beat their swords into ploughshares and their swords into pruning hooks . . . a world in which all will respect the dignity and worth of all human personality.[14]

CONNECTION OF THE STORY FORM AND THEMES OF LOVE AND JUSTICE

As the plot unfolded, in many cases, King's vocal talents were more musical and the audience was more receptive and anticipatory. Much of his technique consisted in building upon the main idea with strength and imagination, holding the listener there with very interesting insight and oratory and then moving to an often "surprising" conclusion. In the narrative sermon form, this dramatic ending is known as the "phenomenological move."[15] In this case, a sequence of plotted units culminates the conclusion. Perhaps one of the most striking examples of this is King's "I Have a Dream" speech. A number of very vivid units consisted of America's historical defaults of justice, to expressions of weariness and dissatisfaction of the discriminated, to a charge to keep hope alive, and the culminating unit of a very powerful eschatological vision urged on by all of the previously stated phenomena.

As he addressed issues related to liberalism, King's sermon narrative sought to make connection with the ongoing cause and struggle for equality. When applying the narrative sermon, King generally sought to stress the importance of struggle and perseverance. In a sermon preached during the genesis of the Montgomery bus boycott, he sought to strengthen the hearts and dignity of persons seeking their justice under the law. He pressed the issue of self-dignity by means of Christian and acceptable ways. The sermon was entitled "The Most Durable Power" and had this directive:

> As you struggle for justice, let your oppressor know that you are not attempting to defeat or humiliate him, or even pay him back for injustices that he has heaped upon you. . . . With this attitude you will be able to keep your struggle on high Christian standards.[16]

Garth Baker-Fletcher finds that King's intentionality in this regard was very pointed:

> King saw this struggle as one that had to have the appropriate "attitude," which he labeled repeatedly as "high Christian standards." The application of these high Christian standards to the boycott enabled the Negroes of Montgomery, under King's leadership, to attain a new, higher, and more ennobled view of themselves . . . They were gaining a deeper sense of dignity.[17]

It was King's contention that when persons felt better regarding themselves, their quest for justice was greater. As long as persons were reluctant to protest and to accept "business as usual," their own personal sights had not been lifted. If people were willing to accept their positions of injustice as mere fate, it was a general indication that they had given up on the system. This is a major reason why King's effectiveness was so important. His preaching helped persons to realize that they, even in their humble state, could effect change.

THE BIBLE AS A SOURCE AND AS CENTRALITY FOR MARTIN LUTHER KING JR.

King's expositions on love and justice were generally informed by his understanding of biblical principles. Moreover, a significant portion of his references to dreams and hopes for unified justice were based on very unique exegesis and interpretations of texts on the same. King possessed the ability to apply the narrative form to scripture in a way that was both interesting and exciting. He gave the text a sense of "life" and enticed one to follow the sermon with anticipation. His biblical narration was so meaningful because he took biblical hermeneutics very seriously when speaking to both black and white audiences. Biblical authority and directives gave him a force and impetus to demand justice in the name of a God who was no respecter of persons. The colorful and powerful expositions based on texts from the Bible were an added asset to his effectiveness. Carl Marbury gives this observation:

> Those persons fortunate enough to hear King preach or those who have read some of his published sermons know well that he spoke with "Biblical authority" and as one who "stood under the scriptures." He was not content to merely quote scripture . . . but was concerned to interpret integrously. He was fully capable of moving around in the Bible with confidence and idiomatic ease. . . . King's rhetoric was of the Biblical vernacular.[18]

The source of the scriptures combined with the ideas of other theologians presented us a matchless presentation of ideals and oration. With a talented and directed use of biblical text, King found ways to present justice concerns with authority and to call for righteousness as a part of justice. The biblical narrative was a major spring of King's theological flow of wisdom. He used the biblical narrative in the sense of authority as captioned by Donald McKim in his description of the biblical narrative:

> Theologians who concentrate on this approach [biblical narrative] find examples of narrative texts in Scripture and seek to answer how these texts function as "authority" in the life of Christian communities. Biblical scholars have long been aware of the role of historical narratives in Scripture. These form what some refer to as . . . "salvation history" throughout the Bible.[19]

OLD TESTAMENT HERMENEUTICS

King used this authority of the Bible to question actions of history as well as to search for repentant spirits of equality. In the spirit of Micah, the Old Testament prophet, he often preempted a homily with Micah's burning question:

> What does the Lord require you but to do justice, love mercy, and to walk humbly with your God?—Micah 6.8

As a part of many of his sermons on justice one could hear the very familiar cry of Amos:

> Let justice roll down like waters and righteousness like a mighty stream.—Amos 5:24

In a very radical address to the Southern Christian Leadership Conference (SCLC) entitled "Where Do We Go from Here?" there was a personification of the Old Testament prophet as King made reference to the text regarding the urgency to remain "dissatisfied" over unjust ideals:

> Let us be dissatisfied. Let us be dissatisfied until every state capital houses a governor who will do justly, who will love mercy, and who

will walk humbly with his God. Let us be dissatisfied until from every city hall, justice will roll down like waters and righteousness like a mighty stream . . . until the lion and the lamb shall lie down together, and every man shall sit under his own vine and fig tree.[20]

A particular level of conscious raising is appealed to here based on a typology of biblical motif. Prophets could never become "satisfied" with injustice. Thus, persons are lifted to a sense of awareness based on biblical example. While this theologian had extreme exposure to the likes of Tillich, Davis, Buber, Nygen, Niebuhr, and so many thinkers who were outside of the realm of traditional African American religion, when it came to relating to the "brothers and sisters," he generally focused on the Bible. Hence, as was the case with much African American folk theology, much of his preaching was centered on the basic theology of the Old Testament. Civil Rights issues and justice concerns touched the very fiber of being of those affected. As it was the case with Old Testament prophets, justice was a pastoral issue and not just a political issue. In an outline that suggests the basic tenet of pastoral care issues in Old Testament theology, G. M. Tucker presents a summation of Old Testament guides that are helpful in issues of pastoral support. I find that this particular list is not only helpful in the understanding of King's reading of basic covenant theology, but also presents guidelines for biblical foundations for justice:

1. One should neither take for granted nor overlook the obvious theocentric character of Biblical thought . . . and that any concern for the care of others will be lived out in the context of divine care.
2. Human beings are not only creatures but children of God, and destined for covenantal relationship.
3. Biblical care is communal and corporate, not individualistic.
4. Given the historic and even physical concreteness of Biblical thought . . . life in its historical particularity is taken with ultimate seriousness.

5. Old Testament thought knows of a relationship between God and people that allows for the free and full expression of all feelings . . .

6. Biblical means of care are by no means limited to one form of response but are diverse.[21]

These six points are an excellent summation of King's normative understanding of Old Testament theology. He often uplifted the Exodus saga as a sign of hope and encouragement. Truth was realized in the firm belief that the God of justice always: 1) cared for God's own; 2) remained a presence in times of struggle; and 3) called oppressors to task. Richard Lischer observes:

> [H]e [King] reads the Exodus and all his favorite texts with two voices. One is the voice of liberation, which promises the ultimate victory of his people; the other is the voice of prophetic critique, which discerns in the triumph of God the defeat of God's enemies. He [King] does not choose two words with which to make these distinctions, but two tones of the one Word.[22]

The "Word" is filled with ideals of God's divine justice, human worth and dignity, and a strong sense of urgency. All of these issues were so characteristic of the Old Testament prophets. Witness this Word in a paragraph from "Death of Evil":

> When the Israelites looked back all they could see was here and there a poor drowned body beaten upon the seashore. For the Israelites, this was a great moment. It was the end of a frightful period in their history. The meaning of this story is not found in the drowning of the Egyptian soldiers, for no one should rejoice at the death or defeat of a human being. Rather, this story symbolizes the death of evil and of inhuman oppression and unjust exploitation.[23]

King was a marvel at using Old Testament narratives and formulas to bring about a change of outlook and encouragement for so many persons. It was a very unique interpretation and personification of justice texts. Like many African American preachers, he did not merely use the Bible texts for literary reference, but he allowed the Bible to "use him." Further, the unspoken goal (of preaching) is an intuitive *experience* of the Word which is planted deep in human consciousness.[24] In this regard, he planted many motifs of liberation and hope for a new land of equality. Very reliant upon the Exodus experience, King's preaching of Old Testament texts was presented with conviction and the power of a personified Moses. Nowhere was this ideal more vivid than in his "I've Been to the Mountaintop" speech:

> Well, I don't know what will happen now. We've got some difficult days ahead. But it doesn't matter with me now. Because I've been to the mountaintop. And I don't mind. Like anybody, I would like to live a long life. Longevity has its place. But I'm not concerned about that now. I just want to do God's will. And He has allowed me to go up to the mountain. And I've looked over. And I've seen the Promised Land.[25]

Such eschatological hopes were paramount to the Exodus tradition. Since God was a just God, the idea was that all would achieve a state of justice when God so directed it. The preaching of King interpreted the strong hope that wrong would be turned "inside out" and that at the right and proper time "truth crushed to earth will rise again." His pronouncements about God were always inclusive and his statements regarding God's judgments were generally binding. As was the case with most Old Testament prophets, announcements of God's judgment may sometimes yet carry opportunity for expeditious repentance. In the "I Have a Dream" speech, he called upon America to repent while there was still time:

> Now is the time to make justice a reality for all God's children. It would be fatal for the nation to overlook the urgency of the moment. This sweltering summer of the Negro's legitimate discontent will not pass until there is an invigorating autumn of freedom and equality. . . . The whirlwinds of revolt will continue to shade the foundations of our nation until the bright day of justice emerges.[26]

King's Old Testament construct bore also values of universality that were realized in his global visions of peace and monotheistic values of the human person and the human condition. Central in this view of the human condition was God's awareness of peril and pain and a love for the natural unity of the created order.[27] In this regard, justice is inevitable.

New Testament Hermeneutics

We noted that the Exodus saga was a prevailing theme of King's Old Testament hermeneutics. It is safe to assert that the basic foundation for his New Testament sermonic construct was the love ethic of Jesus, with specific directives found in the Sermon on the Mount. Based on the teachings of Jesus, King preached a powerful and radical love ethic that consisted of love for the oppressor. This foundation of radical love became the basis for the Civil Rights revolution. King's preaching carried many strong edicts for universal love that were driving forces in the quest for justice. The ability to love one's enemy was a cleansing source for persons to move on to a higher plane of expectation and living. This, of course, was a very different construct compared to the content of many African American preaching greats who preceded him in history. Such preachers as Nat Turner, David Waller, and Henry Highland Garnet drew attention to vivid themes of apocalyptic wrath, slavery selling (Joseph), the so-called Curse of Ham, and strong references to Ethiopian redemption. Instead, King focused on the love of Jesus and how the internalization of this love would prove to be a revolutionary force in human history. This was an unprecedented teaching of a significant historical African American preacher![28]

King was influenced by teaching traditions of Crozer Seminary that insisted on the basic person and message of Jesus for sound preaching. As the content of his preaching career began to develop, it would be obvious that he would not alter this teaching. Using the premise of love, persons began to hear stirring homilies on the basic tenet of the Christian gospel—agape love. Moreover, it was this unique understanding of the centrality of love that gave a sense of purpose, unity, organization, and stability to the justice movement.

What made King's interpretation of New Testament love so different from these homileticians who had gone before him? Certainly, many had called for persons to love in the Christlike manner. Social gospel clergy called for a sense of societal responsibility in rebuilding a state of trust for the nation. This, they alluded, could only be done by sincere "brotherhood" on all levels of society. Niebuhr maintained that the connection between morality and power could be less complex if there existed a state of pacifist or nonviolent quest. Theories of personalism began to draw attention to the possibilities of the power of a personal God for a state of uninterrupted divine love. Nevertheless, even though influenced by these ideals, King found that a very strong connection between love and justice was necessary. This was the major departure of his teaching of New Testament love. During the beginning of the Montgomery bus boycott, King presented this premise during his address:

> I want to tell you this evening that it is not enough to talk about love. Love is one of the principal parts of the Christian faith. There is another side called justice. . . . Justice is love correcting which would work against love. . . . Standing beside love is always justice. And we are only using the tools of justice.[29]

Noting the importance of this love/justice connection in the theology of King, James Cone goes on to make a very important observation:

> I emphasize the theme of justice as King's starting point. . . . No interpreter of King has identified justice as the primary focus of his thinking at the start of the Montgomery Boycott. Most are so eager to stress love as the center of his thoughts and actions [as King himself did when he reflected on the event] that they [like King] fail to note that this was a later development in his thinking.[30]

As King grew stronger in the ministry of the movement, we began to hear not just teachings of nonviolent resistance, but a keen sense of the love/justice motif. This is why he often appealed for universal cooperation and concerted efforts. It was one thing for supporters of Civil Rights to do something for the movement, but it was an entirely different aspect when a full understanding of justice was applied and these same supporters did something with the movement by joining body and soul.

The love of enemy was a potent force in the understanding of the dynamics of justice. If persons were able to love those who set forth despising methods of injustice and disregard, those same persons put forth a reminder of God's judgment by not hating them or by not reciprocating the evil. In this process, strength was also realized by the victims who found a source of justice in their very ability to love the enemy:

> To our most bitter opponents we say: We will match your capacity to inflict suffering by our capacity to endure suffering. Do to us what you will and we will still love you. . . . Throw us in jail and we will still love you. One day we will win freedom, but not only for ourselves. We shall also appeal to your heart and a conscience that we shall win you in the process, and our victory will be a double victory.[31]

King's narration of New Testament texts carried a strong resemblance to Christological love. He exemplified this aspect as he remained loyal to traditional teachings of African American religion regarding the teachings of Jesus. Very often he refers to the "Lily of the Valley," the "Bright and Morning Star," and many other set Christological references out of the African American preaching tradition. While he was well-versed in the intellectual liberal tradition, King often mixed his cultural background with the intellectual. While he often deliberated on love/justice with many references to liberal theologians, he ended or highlighted many sermons in the Christological tradition of African

American preaching. Note the very dramatic ending of "Loving Your Enemies":

> But the empire of Jesus, built solidly and majestically on the foundation of love, is still growing. It started with a small group of dedicated men, who, through the inspiration of their Lord, were able to shake the hinges of the Roman Empire, and carry the Gospel into all the world. Today, the vast earthly Kingdom of Christ numbers more than 900,000,000 and covers every land and tribe. Today we hear again the promise of victory:
> Jesus shall reign where'er the sun
> Does his successful journeys run
> His kingdom stretches from shore to shore
> Till moon shall wane and wax no more.
> . . . Jesus is eternally right.[32]

In traditional African American preaching, the theme of love is paramount. In spite of difficulties, hate, or despair, the central message is that Christ is love. Since Christ is love, victory is always an expectation. Combined with his own special theology of non-violent resistance, King had a manner of combining victory themes with themes of love. This was *not* foreign to African American preaching. William Watley observes:

> It is possible that one of the reasons King so readily appropriated the love motif in Gandhism is that love is one of the great themes of traditional black preaching. . . . Traditionally, black preachers have been aware of how easily hate can grip and harden the hearts and spirits of black people. . . . Therefore King may have had a natural inclination to identify with the love ethic of Jesus in traditional black preaching and fostered and demonstrated this in the black church.[33]

Another important messianic aspect of King's preaching was a sense of hope. If Christ was love, then, as King so often alluded, there was always hope in spite of everything. His echoes of encouragement and bright outlooks were often based on the content of the New Testament. Many of the eschatological visions expressed hope and gave encouragement to the disinherited. As he would often chide for courage in the struggle, there was always a reminder that "unearned suffering is redemptive." Hence, even with heavy crosses, there was still hope. The cross of Jesus was very significant in his interpretation of New Testament theology. This was very much in keeping with the African American Church. He often referred to his leadership as his "cross." Nevertheless, he found a sense of hope—even with the crosses. This is what the black church has preached for generations. Cone sums these major issues of King's New Testament hermeneutics:

> Justice, love, and hope—these three themes shaped the heart of King's faith and theology. Each theme must be interpreted in the light of Jesus' death on the cross. The centrality of the cross for King's faith is what separated him from liberal theology and placed him solidly in the heart of the black religious tradition.[34]

KING'S MASTERY OF TRADITION OF IMAGINATION IN PREACHING

Theological Imagination

As most African American traditional clergy, King was a master of the use of sermonic imagination. Imagination is a spiritual way of "knowing" that transcends logic and actual reality. Thus, expressions are informed by "spiritual" sources. This tradition in preaching has had a lasting effect on the church. When persons were not versed in formal theologies, they were guided by a spiritual perception of the world. Most of the time, these imaginations were colorful, lively, and very encouraging. In that spiritual truth and revelation were involved, imagination was not always pleasant. There are times when it is necessary to paint a divinely-inspired picture that may be vivid, but not always joyful.

King, as most clergy of the tradition, had the unique ability to put color and vitality to various concerns by use of prophetic imagination. Paul Wilson maintains that there are three basic types of sermonic imagination: prophetic (discerning), ethical (community oriented), and poetic (interpretive).[35] In each category, we find that King was very fluent with sound theology. Before giving specific examples of his use of imagination, I offer the following chart to suggest major points of departure that are found in King's oral imagination as compared to the real-life situations that he was forced to address:

Perceived Real Issues	King's Spoken Imaginative Theology
Physical dwellings	Spiritual dwellings
Human-directed universe	Divine interventions in cosmos
Set limitations for justice	Removal of justice limits
Life's ongoing despair	Life's hope for oppressed
Consternation	Celebration and Promise
Existent mortality	Soulful visions of peace
Selfish motivations	Empathy for all
Hatred/separation	Love/unity of purpose
Chaos as norm	Creativity as norm
Academic formula	Biblical revelations
Political boundaries	Eschatological hopes

Prophetic Imagination

Prophetic imagination offers an alternative to the way things simply "are" and the way in which God "intends" that they should be. With a very strong foundation of biblical text, this idea detangles limitations set by humanity regarding God's will and poetically offers aspirations that transcend human boundaries. In this regard, preaching is captivated with musings of extreme possibility and does not accept anything that falls short of God's sovereignty. Preaching in the African American tradition has long been dominated by the limitless love of God that moves beyond any type of imagined or imposed visions. King was no exception to this rule of thought. His dramatic preaching was often dominated by a theology of love, possibility, and justice for all. He dared to imaginatively open these doors that time had closed for so long. It was his summation that God willed a particular order of the universe, since the formation of the human race, that could not be altered by persons. Even if it did not occur until some envisioned futuristic moment, God's will would be realized. He was especially convinced that justice was a vital part of this divine will. Hence, so many sermonic references allude to this type of imagination. In the sermon "A Tough Mind and a Tender Heart," note the prophetic imagination of assurance that concludes the sermon:

> At times we need to know that the Lord is a God of justice. When slumbering giants of injustice emerge in the earth, we need to know that there is a God of power who can cut them down like the grass and leave them withering like the green herb. . . . When days grow dark and nights grow dreary, we can be thankful that our God . . . will lead us through life's dark valleys into sunlit paths of hope.[36]

In so many instances, King's sermons ended with very memorable prophetic imagination of a renewed universe and lovelier dwelling with God's providential care ushering in a realm of peace. This was so much in the African American preaching tradition. Note also the conclusion to an address entitled "Where Do We Go From Here" delivered to the SCLC:

> Let us realize that the arc of the moral universe is long but it bends toward justice. Let us realize that William Cullen Bryant is right: Truth crushed to earth, will rise again . . . with this faith we will be able to sing in some not too distant tomorrow with a cosmic past tense, "We have overcome, we have overcome, deep in my heart, I did believe we would overcome."[37]

Walter Brueggemann finds that a major task of prophetic ministry consists not just in the process of nurturing and nourishing, but in evoking a "consciousness and perception alternative" to the existing dominant culture that surrounds us.[38] With his values on love and his skillful delivery of these issues, King was effective in instituting various levels of alternative perceptions of culture. Of course, he did not change the hearts and minds of many. Nevertheless, one must agree that the culture's ideals were improved markedly by his contributions and oration. The famous "I Have a Dream" and "I've Been to the Mountaintop" speeches are great examples of prophetic imagination.

ETHICAL IMAGINATION

Ethical imagination supposes a sense of compassion and seeks to bring persons to a level of mutual respect. Responsible living and admiration of others are appealed to in this type of imagination. For King, it was essential to press the fundamentals of the New Testament love ethic and to always uplift the dignity of all persons. So often the preacher-theologian presented vivid moral indictments to call attention to biblical and legally abused covenantal boundaries that held precedence for unified goals. King's preaching carried a concern for the moral character and convictions of individuals and the collective society for justice implications. A particular concern(s) was identified, and the sermon was developed in a very imaginative manner to address particular issues. In this regard, the mind is opened to many ethical possibilities once the major concerns have been identified. As mentioned in the earlier discussion regarding sermonic imagination, visionary and authoritative aspects are employed in a contextual manner. The tradition of preaching in the African American church has a history of placing concerns, ideas, and situations in a very memorable form to draw on central images.

Ethical imagination was a useful manner in which King pressed major thematic and vivid concerns into the minds of listeners.

(This, of course, was done with skillful biblical interpretation.) King's preaching carried very crucial ethical implications for social action. Since preaching, in general, is evangelism, the ethical imagination employed by King was indeed a form of evangelism for justice. Enoch Oglesby makes the following observation pertaining to King's theology:

> Concretely speaking, the idea of evangelism in the thought of King is that evangelism is the "good news" of the Gospel of Jesus Christ shared among us, for us, and in behalf of God's liberating activity on the world. Evangelism as social action, therefore, brings together three important clues in the life and faith of the church. The first clue is the recognition that the God of the Bible is *a sending God.* . . . the second is [that] God is a healing God . . . the third clue of evangelism as social action is . . . *God [is] a liberating-relational God.*[39] (italics mine)

This threefold image of God's activity, as Oglesby suggested, was very important in King's ethical expressions. He used this evangelistic style to encourage the masses, as well as to remind the greater society that God is yet sending forth liberation, in spite of situations of injustice. Note the stern manner of evangelical ethics that is stated in a sermon/address given in front of the Montgomery, Alabama, state capital building in March 1965 defending a march for voting rights, in spite of difficulty from state troopers:

> The battle is in our hands in Mississippi and Alabama, and all over the United States. For all of us today the battle is in our hands. The road ahead is not altogether a smooth one. . . . We must keep going. . . . We will be able to change these conditions.[40]

Indeed, we are indebted to King's imaginative theology for so many expressions of liberation and theologies of hope. As one who is very compassionate about his theology, his deep feelings of conviction often illuminated his sense of imaginative communication.

In the 1957 sermon "The Birth of a New Nation," he relates a trip to Ghana and his meeting with Prime Minister Kwame Nkrumah in celebration of that nation's independence from Britain. In the course of the sermon, he admits his high level of emotion as he compares colonialism in Africa to segregation in America. One can feel his prophetic and ethical imagination coming together:

> There seems to be a throbbing desire, there seems to be an eternal desire for freedom within the soul of every man. [When the new flag went up] I started weeping. I was crying for joy. I could hear that old Negro spiritual once more crying out, "Free at last, free at last, Great God almighty, I'm free at last!"[41]

At this point, his spiritual imagination had informed him that if God had done this for the Africans, then God would surely do this for the Africans in America.[42]

SACRED POETRY

A major trait of African American traditional preaching is the flowing creativity of words and powerful image. Evans Crawford makes this observation:

> The preacher does not merely want to say, speak, or articulate the Word. The preacher seeks to "sound" the Word so that people not only "hear" but also "see" it. . . . Essentially, the Israelites were an "ear" people. The first word of the Shema was "hear," not "see."[43]

When it comes to basic worship, African Americans, in general, are "ear" people. It is very important to hear the Word and to be able to formulate spiritual images within the soul. The creativity of the sermon is a "joint effort" between the hearers and the speaker. Hence, the skill of the craft is to design audible theology that is capable of imaging. Poetry, images, and other spiritually sensory forms are always helpful for persons to witness. In the tradition of black preaching, poetry and poetical moves are essential in the sermon dynamics. It yet remains that the best sermons are sermons that are not only "heard," but are "seen" as well. The use of various forms and figures of speech are illuminations for clarity and power.

When King approached a pulpit or podium, poetry and spiritual imaging would begin to flow. No only was this in keeping with forms of the tradition, but his skill in poetical reference enhanced the discipline of preaching. His poetry of justice and liberation was effective in moving persons to act on and to respond to the message with a positive and enlightened attitude.

HERMENEUTICAL METAPHOR

As mentioned, King embodied the African American preacher in an expert and outstanding use of metaphor in preaching. Metaphor brings a particular issue or concern to life by the use of comparative language and image. Generally, the image used represents a major idea or intended concern. Metaphor uses an image from one realm of thought to stand for some other concern or thought. ("The Lord is my shepherd"; "God is an eagle.") This was a special feature of King's orality. He could awaken images within persons to grasp a message of new vision and possibility. King loved to relate justice concerns and injustice indictments to metaphor. This form as employed by black preachers is characterized by reusable picture language also known as metonymy.[44] King's memory is endowed with such fixed metaphors as:

The mountains of despair	Long, shameful corridors of time
Dark night of injustice	Dark valleys/sunlit paths
Tranquilizing drug of gradualism	The Promised Land of freedom
Daybreak of justice	

In the sermon "A Knock at Midnight," again one hears the metaphor of "midnight" with a progression of thought development linking various points of concern that have a "midnight" motif. Based on the Lukan parable, he sets the tone for the midnight metonymy:.

> Although this parable is concerned with the power and persistence of prayer, it may also serve as a basis for our thought concerning many contemporary problems and the role of the church in grappling them. It is midnight in this parable; it is also midnight in our world, and the darkness is so deep that we can hardly see which way to turn.

He goes on to outline metaphorically concerns of "midnight" in the following areas:

1. The social order
2. Humanity's collective life
3. The moral order
4. Racial segregation
5. War

Nevertheless, like all midnights, these pass away, and there is hope for the dawn:

> Disappointment, sorrow and despair are born at midnight, but morning follows. "Weeping may endure for a night," says the Psalmist, "but joy comes in the morning." This faith adjourns the assemblies of hopelessness and brings new light into the dark chambers of Pessimism.[45]

Particularly in issues of social unrest, segregation, and injustice, King used the power of metaphor to call attention to such concern. It is very clear that justice themes and hopes remain a metaphor even today. An excellent example of metaphor on a justice theme is the "I Have a Dream" speech. In this case, varied metaphors combine to present a hope for justice, as well as a chastisement on the nation for long delaying the justice process. This speech remains a favorite and perhaps most memorable because of the very lively and activating images and metaphors. Communication specialist Martha Solomon suggests that King, in this instance, combines a matrix of metaphoric speech that made the "dream" such a significant art. She suggests the following scheme:

> Within the speech [Dream], King develops three extensive images: 1. the Constitution as a promissory note [approx. 170 words], 2. the dream of achieved racial justice [approx. 290 words], and 3. the "ringing out" of freedom throughout the country [approx. 220 words]. These images constitute a substantial portion of an address of about 1,600 words.[46]

The suggestion is that these three major issues present a reminder of the constitutional guarantee of rights, a defaulting of the country on such a guarantee to all, and a hope for a unified vision. It is interesting to observe the power of metaphor. In this speech, the power of vision is very prevalent. In addition, a heightened awareness of national issues regarding justice takes form.

King had the ability to combine biblical metaphor with social issues to stress a given concern. We have previously mentioned the metaphor of the Exodus, the Pharaohs, and others from Old Testament images. He was very responsible in presenting biblical images as metaphor. We find that they were very effective. In the previously mentioned sermon "Death of Evil,"delivered in 1956 at St. John the Divine Church in New York, the metaphorical matrix is focused on "evil." Evil represented political oppression, death of the human spirit, and moral oppression. Based on the crossing of the Red Sea, evil was compared to the "Pharaohs" of hatred and strife:

Within the wide arena of everyday life we see evil in all of its ugly dimensions. We see it expressed in tragic lust and inordinate selfishness . . . in high places . . . in imperialistic nations . . . clothed in the garments of calamitous wars. . . . [47]

Of course, he ends the sermon with a hope that the light of faith will lead us from the dark of evil. The use of biblical metaphor was a great favorite with King (Pharaohs, Promised Land, Mercy Seat, New Day). This was also in keeping with basic homiletical theory. Mitchell states:

Jesus used a great many types of figures of speech in his preaching and teaching. It was effective because it was simply a familiar, striking parallel to experiences common in an agrarian society. Figures clarify and illuminate; they also motivate by providing identification.[48]

As King preached justice and equality, the relating of these issues via preaching metaphor can never be taken for granted. Under the naked eye, those images became a part of our thinking and rethinking about the church's mission for equality. David Buttrick makes this point regarding metaphor:

Metaphors are more important than we know; they orient our ethical thinking. Behind our behavioral selves are systems of related metaphors, or better, models made from congruent metaphors.[49]

Hence, the beauty of King's poetry carried many implications for social concerns and global justice that are a part of our vernacular to this day. This is especially true in the case of nonviolent ethics. As many authors have prolifically stated, the words of King have been great incentives to review the church's mission for global peace and unity. The gifts of his many metaphorical matrixes and symbols remain very important reminders of the tasks yet to be done. By his powerful and poetic articulation of a driving conviction of liberation, the African American church became aware of a capacity to effect change and to "overcome."

RHYTHM/CADENCE

A persistent element of the black preaching form is the component of rhythm and repetition. Akin to African culture, these traits are celebrated as very important and lasting forms of oral sacred communication. King was very skilled in recounting this quality. He was able to maintain a steady flow of effective communication by employing a particular rhythmic pace which contributed to the uniqueness of his oral delivery in public speaking and in preaching. Ideals, images, and powerful thoughts on justice and freedom were driven into the minds of his hearers with lasting pursuance.

The repetition of words and phrases that occur in successive sentences has always given spiritual excitement to African American folk preaching. This concept, technically known as anaphora, dominates many of King's sermons. Robert Harrison and Linda Harrison made the following observation:

> There are numerous examples of anaphora in King's speeches. For example, in "On Police Brutality," the phrase "If you can accept it . . . " emerges at the beginning of several sentences. In his "We Shall Overcome" speech, "We shall overcome because . . . " is repeated. In the "How Long? Not Long?" speech, King returns to "How Long? Not Long." Along with the first repeated lines of "I Have a Dream . . .," "We can never be satisfied . . .," "Go back to . . .," and "With this faith . . .," King says, "Let freedom ring . . ." at least eleven times. . . . [50]

There is a spiritual empowerment that accompanies the ringing of repeated phrases. The spoken exigency presses a prayerful awareness into the hearts of persons. To this day, African American clergy maintain this unique tradition of sermonic repetition. Lischer and other scholars maintain that there are at least five dominant forms of sermonic repetition that were found in King's preaching:

1. **Alliteration**—the first sound of several words is repeated. ["We have come here today to cash a check."]
2. **Anaphora**—repetition of same word or groups of words. ["Let freedom ring" . . . "Let freedom ring."]
3. **Assonance**—similar vowel sounds followed by different consonants. ["That mag-ni-ficent tril-ogy of dura-bi-lity."]
4. **Epistrophe**—repetition of words or same group of words at the end of successive clauses. ["In spite of the difficulty, I have a dream." . . . "I still have a dream."]
5. **Amplification**—repeating the same point in many different ways, resulting in a unique cumulative effect. [". . . people get tired . . . we are tired . . ."], ["For many years we have shown patience . . ."], ["Now we must protest . . ."][51]

A very striking example that combines a number of these forms occurs during the "Mountaintop" speech. King has related a number of incidents involving threats to his life. In a very emotional manner, he tells of nine dangerous potential stabbings that would have been fatal had he sneezed. King touches the hearts of the audience as he tells of a letter that he received from a little white girl who expresses her joy that he "didn't sneeze." He then takes off on a powerful mixture of poignant repetitive reversal:

And I want to say tonight that I am happy that I didn't sneeze. Because if I had sneezed, I wouldn't have been around here in 1960, when students all over the South started sitting-in at lunch counters. . . . If I had sneezed, I wouldn't have been around here in 1962 when Negroes in Albany, Georgia, decided to straighten up their backs. . . . If I had sneezed, I wouldn't have been here in 1963, when the Black people of Birmingham aroused the conscience of the nation, and brought into being the Civil Rights

Bill. If I had sneezed, I wouldn't have had a chance to tell America about the dream I had. If I had sneezed, I wouldn't have been down in Selma, Alabama. . . . I'm so happy that I didn't sneeze.[52]

In a number of instances, King involved the listener with this poetic involvement through repetitive sound and word. Persons were able to grasp a fond appreciation for his words and to maintain a memory for the same. Of course, the "I Have A Dream" speech echoes with these repeated images and spiritual sounds. It is little wonder why the speech is remembered for certain recurring images:

1. "I have a dream"—nine times
2. "We can never be satisfied"—five times
3. "Go back"—six times
4. "Let freedom ring"—ten times[53]

These forms of sermonic repetition produced a sense of justice litany as persons became involved in the essence of the message. It was very important during that time in our history for discouraged persons to remember those gems of promise and hope. King's method, as a product of the African American church, was on target in performing this need. It was not just the beautiful ring in his plausible tenor voice; but, it was also the comfortable, convincing, and spirited African American religious genre that gave a sense of jurisdiction to his words and form. Hence, King was deemed a prophet and preacher for justice as one from the cultural tradition. Cornel West lends witness to this point:

My claim is that black church viewpoints not only fundamentally shaped King's thought, but influenced the themes and elements he responded to and accentuated his encounters with liberal Christianity . . . In his own writings and sermons, he simply presupposed this influence and always assumed that his being a black Baptist minister spoke for itself regarding this black church influence.[54]

This influence was constantly heard, felt, and read in the thinking and expression of King.

EXAMPLES OF KING'S USE OF BASIC SERMON FOCUS AND TYPE

Homileticians suggest that there are basic forms and genres that constitute categories for effective sermonic action. Based on his uniqueness and versatility, it is difficult to limit King to one particular form. It is safe to suggest that he used a number of traditional sermon types with great effectiveness. Samuel Proctor reminds us of four basic types of sermons: 1) narrative; 2) expository; 3) topical; and 4) thematic.[55] These forms were discussed mostly in our section dealing with the nature of African American preaching. Nevertheless, it is interesting to note that King was a master of all of these forms.

1. **Narrative**—the use of a long scripture passage that highlights a major proposition. Examples: "A Knock at Midnight," "Death of Evil," "The Drum Major Instinct," "The Man Who Was a Fool."
2. **Expository**—a brief passage with close attention to details. Examples: "In a Word," "Give Us the Ballot," "Our God Is Able," "Three Dimensions."
3. **Topical**—sermon is based on an issue of relevant concern with textual support. Examples: "Christmas Sermon on Peace," "A Time to Break Silence," "Love in Action," "Maladjusted."
4. **Thematic**—the use of a dramatic text or theme that resounds throughout the sermon/speech. Examples: "I Have a Dream," "The Most Durable Power," "How Long," "Mountaintop."

CHAPTER FOUR

SAME BREAD — DIFFERENT SOULS

Homiletical Tasks and Existential Challenges of
Preaching Today

IN THE LIGHT OF PREVIOUS DISCUSSIONS regarding the nature and historical significance of the African American preaching genre, it has been suggested that issues of justice are very intentionally found in this content of prophetic preaching. Moreover, one finds that theo-political issues and hermeneutical justice are inextricably bound in the religious interpretations of the African American church. These interpretations present a sense of unification and wholeness with standing hermeneutics that do not segment such issues as confessional salvation, justice imperatives, and the anticipation of the divine liberating act. Given the ongoing social, political, and spiritual challenges that we face, it is imperative that such a balance is maintained and monitored in the preaching content. The constant yearning for "good news," even at the borders of our violent "Red Seas" of life, causes the soul to see that level of assurance that is often generated during the preaching moment. In the light of this exigency and spiritual demand, I suggest a threefold homiletical task for effective preaching in the African American church for this millennium:

1. Celebration
2. Identification of Evil
3. Ongoing Communication and Connections

THE TASK OF MAINTAINING
CELEBRATION IN PREACHING

A crucial task of preaching in the African American church remains that of providing a sense of balance to the reality of worldly stress and the content of the good news. Of course, this content presents an audacity to hope and spaces of comfort that come from the divine mandate to "believe, anyhow." More times than not, this exercise of finding a zone of peace produces opportunity to celebrate. This celebration is based on the aforementioned premise that "God is good all of the time" and "All the time, God is good!" A major emissary of this uplifting herald is that of the sermon.

In our age of science and learnedness, we often forget the exercise of spiritual celebration. The challenge of preaching in this age is to "recover" and to uplift the element of sermonic celebration and to do so with a spirit of responsibility and circumspect.[1] Celebration in preaching is characterized by an emotional experience of witness, awareness, and revitalization that comes as a result of "participation" in the sermon. We mention the term "participation" because the tradition calls for that sense of spiritual involvement of both preacher and pew. The tradition is also convinced that the zealous awareness of this good news is made evident when the Holy Spirit provides an "assist" during the delivery. At this point, the sermon is not just in the possession of the preacher; it becomes the community's sermon. The good news of the gospel is *celebration.* An assurance of the blessings and grace of God, a special presence of divine healing of spirit and body, and a promise that in any circumstance "earth has no sorrow that the love of heaven cannot rectify" is very good news that promotes gladness. Frank Thomas presents an important definition of this celebration:

> Celebration is the culmination of the sermonic design, where a moment is celebrated in which the remembrance of a redemptive past and/or the conviction of a liberated future transforms the events immediately experienced.[2]

The preaching task for today's living yet holds to the discovery of these existential joys and encouragement. All who interpret the gospel in pulpit orality need to be certain that *some* good news is shared and uplifted. We are reminded that from a historical point of view, the African American church is a celebration in oppression. That is, even when life was not very promising, there was a sense of delectation to cling to reminders that "this, too, shall pass" or that "the Lord will make a way, somehow." The content of this anticipated blessing is still an urgent element of the sermon that is taken seriously by those who preach. The design of the celebrative sermon as suggested by Thomas is very much in grasping the genre of the "traditional" African American sermon. He suggests the incorporation of five elements of an "emotional process":

1. Use of dialogical language
2. Appeal to core belief
3. Concern for emotive movement (of the sermon)
4. Unity of form and substance
5. Creative use of reversals[3]

One recalls that this formula has remained central at the heart of the traditional sermon. Despite the presence of strife, we yet must locate the spiritual cords of celebration that are connected to the assurance of God's love and grace. The survival of the African American race has rested very dependently on this assertion. Hence, worship foresees a "grand time" of celebration.

The slave preaching genre captured this element of celebration and also cultivated it into the body of the Negro spirituals. (We have already mentioned this rich religious heritage in the previous chapters.) However, one cannot help but note the intrinsic and therapeutic notion of worship celebration that has been responsible for the instilling of courage, faith, positive identity, and surety. A slave mother is thrown into the pits of disrespect and dehumanization, observes her children also in the center of abuse, and her husband is taken and sold to another plantation—yet, she identifies hope in a God of love. This disinherited soul heard a preacher in the brush harbors of the Invisible Institution preaching that "God cannot be turned around." In an emotional celebration of faith, she went to bed without entertaining any thought of suicide or self-abuse, slept soundly, and woke up the next morning in celebration: "I'm so glad trouble don't last always!"

Our challenge today is to yet locate those gems of promise and grace and to uplift them in this society that constantly yearns for "good news." Preaching ought to make a difference in the way persons perceive the impostors of subduing sociopolitical powers and in the manner in which they perceive themselves as having great possibility.

I am not suggesting that the celebrative element should ignore the reality of the evils of human greed and insidious natures of living by proposing an overarching "pie-in-the-sky" approach to preaching. Yet, I do raise the concern that even with our gifted and blessed learning, as well as our focused theological insights, the sermon *still* needs a hint of celebration and assurance. It should be remembered that the sermon is often the only encouragement that many persons will receive. Celebration, then, also presses a sense of sharing the good news and a magnifying of the inner spirits. As preaching takes place, the task of celebration is to also foster an ownership of this good news that remains an asset of sharing.

Celebrative preaching, then, calls for distinctive lessons of identity. Preaching, as in the tradition of King and others, resulted in a contagious atmosphere of sharing and witness. Buttrick makes a distinction, in this manner, between *in-church preaching* and *out-church preaching*. Note the contrast of concepts:

> Out-church preaching is primarily the task of the laity, those who by Baptism have been ordained to a common, evangelical ministry. If the church is a chosen witness to the resurrection, a servant people with a particular task assigned, namely, preaching good news to the "end of the age", then speaking *out* is the Church's

calling . . . lay people are the primary preachers of God's Word . . .
they speak *out.*[4]

The implication here is that the celebrative nature of the
preached content is made and kept "alive" by those who hear it
with enthusiasm and understanding. Sharing and retelling of the
story enhances the dynamic nature of message. This also means,
of course, that the laity must be *empowered* through the very meaningful and responsible preaching that causes them to take the
spiritual directive "outside" of the sheltered church territory. For
Buttrick, this was the importance and crucial nature of *in-church*
preaching. Effective in-church preaching addresses concerns of
identity hermeneutics and biblical interpretation with such intentionality that it gives a significant meaning to discipleship. Such
an awareness allows for a celebrative style of sharing the gospel.
When these elements are identified during in-church preaching,
persons "know Christ in a new way" and present their witness by
celebrating Christ's presence.[5] The discovery of life's gifts of reversals and "second chances" in the complexities of mortality call
for sermonic rehearsals of this celebrative news. Preaching leg-
end Gardner Taylor puts it in this manner:

> The good news of the gospel is that we have a second chance. How
> futile and barren life would be if this were not the case. With our
> errors and our mistakes . . . our days on the earth would be shrouded
> in despair, except for this one rallying asset. . . . So, there is a dignity
> in our days, and there is a sure sense of the royal order to which we
> belong as the sons and daughters of God.[6]

That, indeed, is very good news. Preaching shares the truism
that grace does offer an alternative to the negative impostors of
defeat. These alternate forces of divine intervention may come
across in the form of a "short term" or expectant promise of providence, or even in a distant eschatological epoch. At any rate, the
good news of the gospel merits celebration.

THE TASK OF IDENTIFYING EVIL AND MORAL IMPERATIVES

The prophetic nature of traditional African American preaching has usually centered on a deep moral conviction. This moral understanding of spirituality informs the preacher of moral imperatives and ethical worldview. The depth of this worldview is connected to ancient African religious systems where human conduct standards, definitions of right and wrong, and customs of community ethics were a vital ethos of the religious understanding of existence. As a matter of fact, Africans believed that morals were bestowed by God at the very beginning of human life. Hence, a certain unchallenged authority exists with ethical interpretation.[7]

There has existed at the heart of African American preaching the charge of "naming evil" and of identifying those forces that are not seen as supportive of the common good. This naming of evil in a hermeneutical mode has presented varying formats and methodologies as they have pertained to the distinct periods of the African American struggle in the United States.

I suggest that while biblical hermeneutics have remained constant in the religious history, the *content* of moral values has been presented with distinct biblical motifs as related to a given particular era. The ethical demands, while similar in nature, have called for historically unique homiletical matter. In other words, the slave preacher used a particular genre of biblical images to show God's disfavor with the immorality of slavery. By the time we approach the 1960s, the sermonic moral content is directed towards a more sophisticated population that still calls for equality. The macro evils seldom change (hatred, lying, greed, disobedience); however, some of the micro evils modulate in form and in magnitude (lynching, discrimination, race hatred). Again, the basic message of Christianity does not change. However, the *content of interpretation* is subject to altering.

The slave preacher employed a hermeneutic of direct judgment and suggested fearful consequences. For example, in the interpretation of a slave sermon that centers upon the Red Sea deliverance in the book of Exodus, David Shannon suggests this exegesis of the preacher's sermon:

> In the former instance the particular (Israel's crossing over) is stressed. God destroyed Pharaoh's army. In the latter, the universal is emphasized. . . . The preacher assists the character of the slave-holder. Pharaoh is the object of his attack.[8]

Slave preachers often presented God as an angry judge who would soon "destroy this wicked race" and institute a kingdom of equality. Since the sermon was credited as having come from God, then, the moral foundations of society were often critiqued with a spiritual prerogative.

The preachers of the political activist genre after the Civil War still "called out" evil ideals and immoral actions. The voices of Rev. Richard Cain, a member of the Forty-fourth Congress; Henry McNeal Turner, African Methodist Episcopal (AME) Bishop, U. S. House of Representatives; Henry Highland Garnett, Reconstruction activist; and many other powerful prophetic voices spoke directly to the evils of their current society. Unlike their counterparts of slavery, theirs was a more *direct and social critique* with a Bible base.

Then the turbulent 1950s–'60s uprooted more prophetic voices who, with a slightly different genre, but the same Bible, also presented crucial critiques of the social order. Again, the evil identification was even more direct. Specifications of issues, persons, and situations of injustice often were the very content of the authoritative preached word. (The leadership of Martin Luther King Jr. helped to foster this very effective religious atmosphere and helped to shape a lasting canon for sermonic social critique.) The importance of this era is unmatched in the history of preaching in America. Not only did King assist us in the process of identifying those societal forces of evil intent, but he helped the church to boldly uphold gospel mandates of justice with a strong sense of biblical authority. James Childs purports an important observation regarding this role of African American preaching:

> Our conversations with African-American Christianity offers more than a resource for better understanding of the race issue. The African American preaching tradition is a theologically rich tradition from which we can all draw inspiration and instruction. We have only to look at the life and word of Martin Luther King, Jr. and his fellow leaders among the black clergy in the Civil Rights movement to be reminded that in African American preaching, theology, and church life there has never been a divide between salvation and concerns for justice. . . . People live best and are empowered when they are affirmed.[9]

The task, therefore, remains of African American preaching to empower the masses by unashamedly "calling out" the debtors of societal injury. A careful spiritual "ear" is needed to remain alert for such identification of social intrusions and devaluations of human life. In this regard, spiritual direction is just as consequential as biblical interpretation. There is a yearning for the authentic prophetic comportment of the biblical tradition. However, the prophetic cannot be realized without a disciplined path of spiritual exercise. We who preach are empowered when there is a constant search and surety of God's presence.

Before evil can be reckoned with or any determinations of what entities of society are "out of order" according to divine plan, serious introspection is necessary. This is to suggest that the preacher of this millennium must often undergo a process of spiritual introspection and assessment of our own "spiritual levels." If justice, faith, love, peace, and self-critique are elements that make for a "good" world, such attributes are necessary aspirations for all persons of the "cloth." Careful and serious inner calculations often result in a tacit awareness of our own issues of sexism, racism, and classism. It is a fact that effectual empowerment cannot occur through preaching if the "empowerer" is not also empowered. A refusal to adhere to the necessary exercise of introspection can hinder the anticipated outgrowth of empowerment.

Ongoing Communications, Making Connections, and Testing New Grounds of Hermeneutics

A major challenge to modern preaching in the African American church is that of maintaining the traditional effectiveness of spirit and interpretations. Such questions come to mind as:

1. Has the traditional "Bread" (preaching content) begun to vanish from the waters of African American life?
2. Is the telling of the "old, old story" in dire competition with the age of highly secularized reason, the computer age, and a retard of spiritual values?
3. If so, how can we keep open the necessary spiritual connections to reclaim the preaching tradition?

Such concerns uplift the importance of maintaining a sense of spiritual pedagogy and empowerment in preaching. The genre of African American preaching has remained a very important center of values and moral interpretation. The preacher and the sermon remain a central vehicle of moral interpretation. Enoch Oglesby reminds us of this crucial nature of moral guidance and interpretation that is conceptualized in the African American preacher:

> Just as the (African American) church as a whole became the center of social, moral, and spiritual growth among black people on the one hand, the black preacher eventually became the chief moral teacher and theological interpreter of the black religious experience on the other. The (African American) preacher, in no small way, exerts a dominant influence in the lives of the masses of black folk.[10]

Our concern, then, is that the preaching content will remain effective grounds of moral dialogue. This calls for a responsible assessment of both the text and the context of scripture. Coming to a consensus on moral issues involves a special connection of trust on the part of the congregation and that of the Holy Spirit to visit in confirmation of truth and stated interpretations. Again, one is to be aware of the often occurrence of a "double reading" of texts. That is, congregants often accept a "surface" interpretation of scripture as the preacher waxes in the homiletic moment. However, many also seek a "deeper" interpretation and witness by the Spirit that the vocalized ideals are authentic musings of God's mastery. This is what makes the sermon a truly "community" event. The admonition to always "study to show oneself approved" is a resource that allows one to go "deeper" than just the "surface" orality.

The spiritual history of this phenomenon is rooted in what Stephen Breek Reid calls a "hermeneutic of suspicion." This interpretative nature is combined with an intense hope to keep present in the course of life a nonwavering, loyal, and omnipotent force of being. Yet, again, responsible biblical interpretation is a vital force:

> The black church uses a hermeneutics of suspicion because of the way scripture has been used against African Americans in order to support racist policies. The curse of Ham was used (Gen. 9.20–26) by white slave owners to provide divine sanction of slavery. . . . To begin with, they [AA readers of the Bible] should exercise suspicions whenever a text is used to buttress social order. . . .[11]

The other important concern for seeking this stated depth in a scriptural theology has to do with finding and maintaining that traditional moral ground. As the sermon is often a moral evaluation, then the supportive and precise discussion of that text becomes an urgent and serious exercise.

Does this motif detract the crux of celebration? Of course not. The gospel is good news in all situations. When loyalty is given to the authentic spiritual base of the preaching exercise, "the burden" and "the joy" are realized. One can resonate with Henry Mitchell here in regard to two important tasks of African American preaching:

1. To declare the Gospel in the language and culture of the people for effective communication.
2. To be certain that the Gospel speaks to current needs of the people.[12]

As strange as it may appear to many, we must acknowledge that the challenge of determining basic moral/ethical teachings in African American preaching does take into account the changing methodologies and approaches to worship and the changing nature of society and of the traditions of the African American community. Many observers fear the all-important, spirit-centered African American sermon has become too "laid back" in the wake of our current educated and "worldly" population. In many cases, the spiritual anticipation and delivery of the sermon have been reduced to a more sophisticated approach in an attempt to address the countenance of congregant constituents. If this is done in an effective manner with no apology to or deduction of the gospel's content, then this is great. However, if we substitute the gospel's mandate for lines of comfort and social musings, we leave much to be desired. In this regard, Gary Simpson warns against the concept of "comma preaching," which has a tendency to produce a list of "points" that result in a "list" that could become "boring and dysfunctional." The warning here is that contemporary preaching can be exciting if geared toward the emotive element of life. On the other hand, the result could be a reduction of "alliterative descriptions" that are void of the celebration element.[13] Hence, in seeking the moral tasks of preaching, celebrative connections are important.

Another challenge to the traditional African American preaching is the prevalence of the "Mega Church" and the largely populated "Word Church" of the African American community. Many of these mass church community fellowships have become very successful in maintaining large audiences of worship, mission, and unified identities. To be sure, it is feasible to recall a few factors that have affected the old "traditional family church" of the African American community and the stability of the same:

1. Many traditional, family-oriented churches in the AA community are challenged by changing social roles and realities of the AA family.
2. As traditional historical communities undergo population flight, the churches also often face the same exercises and dynamics.
3. The traditional church, because of the frequent fluctuation of members, is not always in a fiscal position to offer the much-needed social services that larger churches can offer.
4. Many African Americans, in this age of "seeking," desire an alternative to the traditional family Christian church.
5. Misunderstandings, discord from traditional churches, spiritual inquisitions, and new territory of worship that is often racially integrated have gained the curiosity and loyalty of younger African American worshipers.

The truth of the matter is that African American traditional preaching just may be, as Robert Franklin notes, "at a crossroad."[14] While more loyal and dedicated, often older, worshipers remain in the tradition, younger worshipers are attracted to an alternative contemporary style of worship. In many cases, the methodology of preaching is based on an engaged lecture style. As a "sign of the times," this approach to worship and to hermeneutics in the African American church of larger proportions is often void of the historically dominant spiritual elements that have remained a bulwark of spirituality for many. This bantam decline of the African American preaching genre presses a challenge to seek to build stronger grounds of theological purpose and to become more intentional in the mission of building personal grounds of faith. In traditional churches, many expressed that they were often preached "at." In the larger contemporary worship houses, the testimony of many is that they are now the recipients of more dynamic and person-building truths; they are now "preached *to*" and not "preached *at.*" As effective as the hermeneutic process may be in this tradition, I concur with Franklin on the following observations (maybe cautions) that he finds in respect to the "Word Church" ideal:

1. These churches represent an alternative to black Christianity.
2. The churches are not monolithic but encompass a variety of communities (Full Gospel Baptist, neo-Pentecostal Methodist, non-denominational, etc.).
3. Such churches engage in very aggressive proselytizing.
4. A gospel of health, wealth, and success is proclaimed. This is quite attractive to younger persons.
5. Leaders of fellowship, if not careful, stand in danger of self-exaltation as messengers of very special divine mysteries. (This causes a dependence of anxious followers.)[15]

Where, then, do we make the necessary connections and ongoing communications of both personal as well as institutional concern that will enhance and keep African American preaching effective at the border of a brand new millennium? New Afrocentric approaches to the gospel have proven to be very effective. Recent studies have proven that this media-oriented, computer-influenced style of preaching *does* reach the hearts and loyalty of many. This preaching genre calls for a very directed sense of substance that is reflected in the holistic effect of the message. A very disciplined method of study and continued reality testing is necessary for an effective preacher of this age. The moral imperative of biblical truth, the divine mandate of justice, as well as the personal edification of the soul, are all possible when the preacher intently seeks a sure ground of holism. If African American preaching is conditioned by society, as Mitchell and others assert, then there calls for an unapologetic model of preaching for celebration, moral evil awareness, and the continued search for connections and divine clues that help to make sense of the complexities of life.

Oglesby, in another volume, suggests a seven-stage model for moral decision making that is akin to African American culture and is biblically based. He refers to it as the "Covenant-Harambee Method." It is detailed in the following stages:

1. Defining the Problem (understanding).
2. Establishing Boundaries (respecting differences, etc.).
3. Hospitality and Hostility (power relationships, naming good/ wrongdoing).
4. Love and Justice (realization that love and justice are prayer-linked).
5. Oral Stories/Cover Stories (idea that sharing of faith stories has a liberation effect).
6. Suffering and Hope (building bridges of hope and not walls of hate; doing the right thing).
7. Freedom and Responsibility (saying what is permissible but taking responsibility for same).[16]

This conception of community moral decision making is an excellent model for effective African American preaching. Moreover, there is a congruent character of the nature of the preaching of Martin Luther King Jr. Each stage represents an important link to the modern challenges and ethical needs that are the tasks and moral directives inherent in African American preaching. Note the uncanny association of King's method of effective preaching and this very useful and functional methodology of moral decision making as suggested by Oglesby. (Keep in mind that the sermon in AA culture is an exercise in moral interpretation.)

ETHICAL PREACHING METHOD OF MLK (A SEVEN-STAGE MODEL OF ETHICAL METHOD BY OGLESBY)

1. **Defining the Problem**—A talent/gift of Martin Luther King Jr. that towered above others was his prophetic gift of calling/

naming evils with a sense of prophetic clarity. Situations of racism and fear were often given a new definition by King. Persons found in him the ability to use the Word and to effectively redefine issues and to restate concerns that resulted in a unified hope and not an ongoing unified fear. A major trait of this methodology was to authenticate the role of divine presence in the situation. King's command of biblical interpretation assisted, in very careful ways, to state fully the problem; to instill a sense of determination; and, at the same time, to maintain a focused unity surrounding that problem or concern.

2. **Establishing Boundaries**—The efficient use of the New Testament love ethic was a central force in the manner of sermonic "turf" establishment and lessons of "differences" as purported by Martin Luther King Jr. He skillfully used biblical texts to reiterate the boundary of love/hate and violence/nonviolence that would make a grave difference in the journey of the "movement." Moreover, the important sermons on "Love of Enemy" themes were quite instrumental in establishing the moral ground of protest. A new lesson of love and of boundary theology was established in the preaching of King. His method was so powerful in this regard that an important lesson was taught through his sermons: When there is love, nonviolence, and respect for the dignity of all, there are no boundaries.

3. **Hospitality and Hostility**—Again, King's reading of the New Testament provided the basis for his method of naming the evils and the good of society. However, there was always a clear distinction in his messages regarding the power of good relationships, across racial lines, and the detriment of hostile racial disunity. His sermons often reminded us of the advantage of living together as "brothers" or perishing together as "fools."

4. **Love and Justice**—The insistence that "God is on our side" was a crucial theological concern of King. His preaching often reflected the lessons that love and justice cannot be separated. Like other traditional African American preachers, he often pressed the divine link of Christian love to that of an understanding that

justice must arise from the same source. Sermons such as "Death of Evil," "Great . . . but," and "Shattered Dreams" all attest to this theology of moral justice and love.

5. **Oral Stories/Cover Stories**—Without question, the preaching of King had a great liberation effect upon the masses. Like the tradition of sermons that helped to shape him, the ability to use scripture in an exciting, understanding, and liberating manner was the mark of his "good preaching." James Cone recently noted:

> The influence of the Black Church and its central theme of freedom and hope can be seen in the language of King's speaking and writing. Everything he said and wrote sounds like a black sermon and not rational reflection. . . . (He did not adopt the style of theological presentation from any of his white theological mentors.) He may have referred to white theologians and philosophers when he needed to explain his views to a white public, but the style of his presentation was unmistakably from the tradition of black preaching.[17]

King's sharing of that gift was very liberating.

6. **Suffering and Hope**—If King's preaching provided any lasting effect upon disinherited persons, it was his gospel of hope. Juxtaposed to a "give up" doctrine, the worst "beatings" (physical and political) were treated as lessons in hope. King's sermons are dominated with many explanations and expectations of redemptive nature as a result of the onslaught of "unearned suffering." King is perhaps the foremost American preacher of the century to present gospel gems and promises in such a provocative manner that produced hope instead of nursing despair. A sense of right action and right process was a prelude to realizing the fruits of this spiritual hope. The ability to love one's enemy, according to King, is a major sign of hope.

7. **Freedom and Responsibility**—King, of course, felt an unquestioning direction of the spirit of God. His claim, as a prophet,

was that of a "trumpet" of justice and conscious. Hence, his preaching content was charged with bold admonitions of justice and audacious exegesis of scripture that faced the "Pharaohs" of his time with divine reckoning. Moreover, his ability, in sermon, to always "speak the truth in love" was often a motivational factor for the misdoers of justice to take a second look.

Again, while Oglesby presents this model as an agency to measure biblical foundations of covenant and Harambee as a backdrop in moral determination, his suggestions provide a helpful paradigm for comparing the moral content of African American preaching. In the process of examining these and other suggestions, it remains evident that the crucial tasks of African American preaching are centered upon celebrating the good news, providing a careful and spirited identification of evil in society (and a responsible warning/action thereof), and to remain open to the Spirit for new enhancements, pedagogy, and direction by the Spirit for an ongoing effectiveness as a preacher. The preacher of today must be completely honest with his/her callings. This means not only to be open to new voices, but loyal to God's Word. This loyalty brings to our spirit the power of the tradition with ongoing clues to interpretive hermeneutics for "such a time as this."

In addition to exciting exegesis sharing, the constant sharing of faith journeys is necessary. This includes those journeys of the many women of the gospel whose stories have not always been as obvious as their male counterparts'.[18] With unified spirits we can maintain African American preaching as a haven of celebration and as a crucial locale of moral interpretation and identification of antikingdom appearances.

CHAPTER FIVE

PREACHING FOR TODAY

A MOST OUTSTANDING CHARACTER OF KING'S sermonic discourse was that of "calling out" and identifying the evils of society that were latent in American Christianity. He employed his gift of biblical hermeneutics to call us to task in the light of justice miscarriages. During the years of slavery and reconstruction, the issues were very clear regarding the "place" of African Americans. As a result, the preacher addressed racial and justice concerns as a part of the general gospel of good news from the oppressed. The issues of life were generally the central message of the sermon. These issues were blanketed with very appropriate biblical texts. Clergy today, in the spirit of King, are called upon to boldly identify issues of evil in our society and to address them in the spirit of a prophet. The "demons" of the new millennium are very similar to the "demons" of the 1950s in an existential manner. However, the complexity is greater. The bad news is that even as a better informed and privileged generation, our preaching does not always fully address the urgent needs of today.

Major Preaching Issues for MLK	*Major Preaching Issues in Today's Society*
Life under racism	Life in compromise
Corrupt legal systems	Working within the system
Hatred/fear of violence	Violence to "self"—race
Black Folk religion	Contemporary approaches to African American Worship

Social chaos	Drug cultures
Moral strength/unity	Declining moral fibers
Prophetic doctrines	Doctrines of compromise
Unity of purpose	Divergent efforts
Need for hope	Need for hope
Ongoing family values	Family breakdown

Hence, the task of African American preaching on the threshold of a new century is to continue to identify the "evils" of society and to address them in a prophetic manner. Samuel Proctor observes the state of affairs for preaching as very crucial:

The demons may have other names, but they are here! The preacher needs to point them out to the people so that they can be recognized and so that the nature of the struggle can be understood. . . . It is clear that the word could easily spread that human nature is hopelessly polluted. The role of the preacher becomes more and more distinct.[1]

While many African American clergy are very appreciative of the tradition, it is apparent that much "compromise" takes place. That is, we do not hear much of the forceful and effective call to witness for justice and human dignity in preaching. Our efforts in this regard can be strengthened by a combination of the Holy Spirit and a stronger awareness of the need to "call out" societal evils. Dwight Hopkins offers the following advice on the matter:

We have seen King define these demonic powers as racism, capitalism, and capitalist war abroad. Thus to enjoy the rights freely given through God's grace—to realize full humanity—entails eradicating systemic evil. To organize toward what it means to be human forces the church to name Satan's activity. Naming evil, then, comprises part of the organizing effort.[2]

African American preaching, then, remains in a state of urgency to "sound trumpets" of awareness for this generation. Prophetic spirits and responsible biblical interpretation are necessary to help identify and to sound their concerns.

Our homiletical task differs today in the fact that this generation is more complex than it was in the preaching days of Martin Luther King Jr. Racism is more covert. Issues of living are made to be more intellectualized with politics. Hence, the spiritual teaching of "inner awareness" is very important. Today's preaching should reflect this need for a serious spiritual inwardness. It is important to note that the task of preaching in the African American culture is complicated also by the breakdown of the family and traditional family values that were so important in the maintenance of this inner spiritual source.

We are yet mandated by the gospel to seek justice and to extend love—even in difficult situations. This is a warning that comes to caution against what King called "gradualism." The new gradualism is in the form of a very comfortable message that is void of challenge and power. The tradition of African American preaching does remain alive in form, yet, the kerygma of justice and peace is very urgent.

Context vs. Content

I have made a strong case for celebrating the heritage of African American preaching. Having identified historical issues and the genesis of various primary forms of the preaching event, I sought to identify King as a major "player" in this preaching tradition. As we summarize these normative and descriptive findings, another very practical concern is raised: How can preaching enhance justice and other concerns of life with intentional content and not just the important form or context?

One cannot escape the fact that style is very important in the African American preaching tradition. The spiritual style of bringing truth and hope to troublesome situations has been a major task of African American preaching. One cannot take for granted the forms of delivery that have been very critical in helping persons to get in touch with those yearnings for affirmation and meaning. The spiritual presentations by black clergy on Sunday mornings continue to bring a sense of hope to the contradictions of life. As in the tradition of King, preaching today must remain focused on a keen sense of moral reality and not just on an emotional presentation. Again, the context for preaching has changed and is challenged each day. The moral complexities are increasing. Hence, there is an expectation that the sermon will address, in a spiritual and in an involving way, the issues of life. Liberation is yet a most critical issue to address in a spiritual and moving form. However, unlike the preaching of previous generations, a warning flag is waved today to remind us of the very central need to both uplift and to transform minds and spirits. This task is achieved by many with distinction. Nevertheless, a population of those delivering this good news does not take *content* as seriously as they take the very *context* and vocal style of homiletics. James Harris sounds a very important warning:

> On any given Sunday, one can hear a meaningful message being heralded from pulpits across the nation. Likewise, there can be heard a lot of hoopla, thunderous and boisterous sound that does not reflect the serious need to engage in Biblical text and the congregation in a dialogue toward transformation and liberation. Ideally, every sermon should be a harbinger of liberation that germinates in the mind of the preacher. . . . Unfortunately, this is not always the case, and the preacher ends up conforming to existing norms within the congregation rather than transforming the listeners.[3]

The preaching event has always served as a vector for urging strength and positive social identity. The preacher was a driving force in the development of new goals, thoughts, and hopes for persons in this sometimes confusing country. Hence, the sermon is the most anticipated aspect in traditional African American worship. The sermon has served as an important intermediary between the harsh realities of suffering and an inherent confidence that victory is possible. It remains a crucial task for those who preach to be certain that these emotional exhortations are also filled with purpose and directed intentionality for transformation. Indeed, life's realities of racial strife, physical survival, violence, and moral decay are emotional issues. Nevertheless, we are called upon, as was King and preachers before him, to direct this emotional motif with Holy Spirit guidance toward a meaningful end.

Henry Mitchell offers this perspective:

> Our first understanding is to practice an irrevocable commitment to high purpose and to the use of appeals directed to the highest emotions. Evoking tears will never be an end in itself . . . Powerful emotional impact should be viewed in the same way one views dynamite. It can be most destructive when not used for the purposes for which it was made.[4]

Black preaching is celebration in the midst of oppression. It is a spoken celebration that life can be rescued from difficulty. This fact makes the purpose of preaching, even in the cultural forms, very crucial. King did not take this fact for granted. We note the intentional, intellectual, and meaningful content of his messages that were delivered in the African American preaching style with moral imperatives.

African American preaching remains an important moral agent. Richard Gula outlines the components of moral agency as follows:

1. Integrity and identity as the hallmarks of moral life
2. Capacities and obligations
3. Institutions
4. Affections (reactions to values)
5. Perspective, intentions
6. Creative imagination[5]

The task and nature of African American preaching address each of these issues of moral agency. Hence, as a moral enabler, the sermonic content is very acute. This is not to suggest that the historical and cultural forms are not important. However, the implication is that liberation should remain a central goal. Harris stresses this point of liberation:

I am suggesting that style and substance are partners in preaching liberation. The way the sermon is preached—the style of delivery, the involvement of body and mind, the engagement of the audience, the rhythmic crescendos and decrescendos of the voice punctuated by staccato cadences and words uttered in musical style—all this to a degree is as important as the substance of what is being said.[6]

Thus, my premise is that in order for African American preaching to remain effective, the content of the message is to remain a priority. The form and style are important elements that are connected to our spiritual heritage and cannot be ignored. Yet, there remains a place for study, preparation, and social awareness that are all necessary to keep a sharp focus for effective moral agency. Martin Luther King Jr.'s legacy remains a shining example of this union of reason and spirit. Thomas Troeger bears witness to this effectiveness:

King's appeal to the landscape of the heart awakened moral rage so that people's energies were engaged to bring reality closer to the ideals of their mythological world. King's preaching was effective because he envisioned for his listeners what might come to be if they lived out the best yearnings and hopes of their hearts.[7]

EPILOGUE

"WHAT THEN SHALL WE SAY TO THESE THINGS?"

There is indeed a grave need for this heavenly bread to be made available for the starving souls of all persons. If the blessedness of African American preaching is to be "seen for many days" of our existence, then our focus is to remain centered upon discipline, unified purpose, intense searchings, and the "yeast" of the Spirit to keep our spirits fresh. The noble examples and lessons that are inherent in the preaching legacy of African American religion were brought closer to us by the sermonic orality of Martin Luther King Jr. He embedded a theology of inevitable hope with spiritual tradition. This was at a time when we stood at the crossroads of justice and needed a "word" of divine authenticity. James Cone observes:

> King's theology was defined by an eschatological hope. God's promise not to leave the little ones alone in struggle. In his sermons, he often spoke of "midnight," "darkness," and the "cross," usually referring to racism, poverty, and war. But in spite of the great difficulties he encountered in fighting these evils, King was certain that we shall overcome "because truth crushed to earth will rise again."[1]

It is with that same hope in the God of indivisible justice and undying love that we continue to cast such sacred "bread" upon the waters of time. Our elders would remind us: "If we are right," then our earnest striving will be seen for "many days."

TESTING THE "WATERS"

Major Influences of Martin Luther King Jr. on Clergy and Theologians

INTERVIEWS/REACTIONS

As a result of this inquiry, I have sought to establish the fact that both the preaching style and the preaching content of Martin Luther King Jr. have held great influence on the continued legacy of African American preaching. Moreover, I have attempted to demonstrate the premise that the "Preacher King," a product of the historical black preacher, was instrumental in the ongoing establishment of a kerygma of justice and morality. King has contributed very effective dynamics to existent homiletical forms in African American religious expression.

The following questions were posed to a select group of clergy consisting of divergent ages, denominations, and faiths. The samples included twelve African American male Protestants, three African American female Protestants, four Caucasian Protestants, three Roman Catholic Priests, and one Jewish Rabbi. The two questions posed were:

1. "As a major theologian of our time, how much of your thinking, writing, or preaching has been informed by Martin Luther King's teachings of justice?"
2. "Martin Luther King Jr. was indeed one of the greatest preachers in American Christianity. Do you find that his unique style and form of homiletics are yet effective today to move persons toward justice goals?"

Of those who answered, these answers were rendered:

QUESTION NO. 1

"King's tapes can still send chills. I wish King was here to preach about Affirmative Action."

"Indeed. Much of my preaching habits were copied from King."

"I still love to listen to Martin and get inspiration for community issues."

"Even though he was kind of 'sexist,' I still am guided very much by his preaching and principles."

"I am not that sure. But I still gain much from his sermon books like *Strength to Love*."

"King is my preaching hero."

"Martin Luther King Jr. taught me how to preach about prejudice from the Bible."

"I can't preach like him—but I sure learned much from him."

QUESTION NO. 2

"You better believe it! If King were here, maybe some of this racial misunderstanding would not exist."

"Yes, King taught the country to 'preach' a living sermon."

"If we could pattern Martin's style, I think that there would be more unity with churches."

"Nobody wants to preach about justice anymore. We need King back here. It's like preaching on 'Hell'—nobody wants to touch it."

"I still think that people, even today, would stop and listen to a Martin Luther King Jr. preach."

"Yes. I felt like Martin was with us at the Million Man March."

Of ten authors and professors of religion that were solicited,
there were five responses:

1 "A great deal. Martin Luther King Jr.'s 'hermeneutics of justice' for Biblical interpretation is a major plank in my own theory
and practice. Richard Lischer's treatment of King has helped
us all. I have even on occasion been accused of 'sounding like
King.' I think it's a compliment. Needless to say, as one who
worked so closely with King and heard him often, I'm sure that
some of his style and even method slipped into my preaching."
2. "Yes! I am saying this in an upcoming book on black preaching. What worries me is that there is a growing tendency by
younger African Americans to be fooled by a 'white right con-
servatism' which is antithetical to King and the tradition that
he represented. (Upcoming book: *The Preaching of Zion: African American Preaching and the Bible.*)"

> Dr. William B. McClain
> Professor of Preaching and Worship
> Wesley Theological Seminary
> Washington DC

1. "MLK was one of the major influences in my becoming a
preacher. When I heard him preach and bring together the
Bible, African American religion, Western philosophy and theology, and the American spirit in ways that moved me to act for
justice—when all this happened I was overwhelmed by what
preaching can mean and do at its best.

That impression continues to haunt me in creative ways, and his
vivid language has in conscious [and probably unconscious ways]
influenced my work on imagination and images in preaching."
2. "We live in a new and different era requiring new styles of public speech. The electronic media, including videos and CD-
ROMS, have and continue to change our perceptual methods

so that the classical rhetoric of MLK would probably need to be updated with new verbal allusions and ways of organizing words. Nevertheless, I am convinced the fundamental character of MLK's approach will never cease to be effective: a heart on fire with a passion for justice and a mind capable of organizing this into stirring language that pours forth with a tonal quality reflecting all the pain and urgencies of the cause."

Thomas H. Troeger
Professor of Preaching and Communications
Iliff School of Theology
2201 South University
Denver CO 80210

1. "Very little! As I shared with Jim Cone as he was preparing his book, *Martin and Malcolm and America*, many of the clergy my age who were undergraduates during the sit-ins were equally affected by the teachings of Malcolm! We heard what Martin had to say, and he did, indeed, shape a lot of our thinking back during the '60s. Equally as important were the hard questions that Malcolm X was raising!

   Malcolm's insights affected our thinking, writing, and preaching just as much as Martin's did! As a matter of fact, when you read the later King and see how his 'dream' had turned into a 'nightmare,' you find more resonance there in terms of where many of the clergy who were undergraduates during the late '50s and early '60s were than you do in the flowery idealism of Martin who did not understand the nature and depth of racism!

   Dr. King's teachings on justice remained 'ideal.' The reality of racism in this country, however, forced many of us to seek other methods of confronting the system, naming the powers, and speaking the truth 'to power!'"

2. "I don't find Martin Luther King Jr. unique! Martin was cut from the cloth of black preaching in this country. When one studies that genre, one finds Martin to be one piece of a long,

continuous, and unending fabric of African American clergy—
male and female—who have given homiletics its shape and tex-
ture within the black tradition.

I find that the style of Martin was a part of a style much older
than Martin and is still effective today in moving persons toward justice goals. It is the same style that was used by David
Walker in the 1800s!

It is the same style that was used by Frederick Douglas, by
Sojourner Truth, by Adam Clayton Powell Sr., and Adam
Clayton Powell Jr. It is the same style that was used by Gardner
Taylor and that was used by both my mother and my father. I
think that that black style of preaching is one of the most effec-
tive forms of moving persons of faith 'toward justice!'

The key in that previous sentence, however, is the word
'faith.' The sermons of King and the style of preaching that
the black church has boasted of for over 200 years is not a style
that reaches persons of 'non-faith!'"

One has to hear a sermon to be moved by a sermon and,
unfortunately, so much of the world in which we live and the
persons whom we are called to serve are not persons who hear
sermons! For those who do listen to preaching, however, this
homiletical style is the best style for moving persons towards
justice goals."

Dr. Jeremiah Wright
Trinity United Church of Christ
Chicago IL
United Theological Seminary
Dayton OH

1. "My thinking, writing, and preaching have been profoundly
informed by Martin Luther King Jr.'s ideas concerning justice
and his efforts to translate those ideas into practical reality. Dr.
King taught me that written and oral discourse must address
the pain predicament of the poor and oppressed in order to

be authentic. From Dr. King's writings and activities, I learned that the committed life is the best and most ideal life, and I have tried to reflect this in my efforts to educate people through my scholarship and preaching. Dr. King taught us that the scholar and preacher must also be an activist, a point that we so often forget in the academy and in the church. In keeping with this idea, I have always been determined to address the existential realities of black people in my writing and preaching."

2. "A lot of young preachers have adopted King's preaching style and form of homiletics because they speak to concrete human situations. King always addressed the pain predicament of humans in his preaching, and his sermons were designed to stimulate creative thinking and to move people to action around the problems that prevent them from realizing the fullness of their potential under God. This homiletical style and approach is so desperately needed today in a world still afflicted by racism, sexism, poverty, and war."

Dr. Lewis V. Baldwin
Associate Professor
Religious Studies
Vanderbilt University
Nashville TN

1. "My thinking, writing, and preaching are all informed by King's teachings on justice. My first effort to think systematically about this subject was a paper I wrote while in seminary on his concept of justice. Since that time I have always required my students in Christian social ethics to read King's writings. I have written about King's notion of justice in my book, *Empowerment Ethics for a Liberated People*, where I also raise critical questions about his suitability as a model for Christian ethics. On numerous occasions I have preached sermons for the King holiday where my emphasis has been upon justice. In fact, just this past Sunday I preached at my own church on Biblical justice in the

prophecy of Amos, and noted that King's reflections on justice in Amos 5:24 were as important as his declaration that 'I have a dream' in the sermon he preached at the 1963 March on Washington. It goes without saying that this sermon is the most significant statement of a public theology of justice in our time. See my analysis of King's preaching as ethical transcript in Callen, *Sharing Heaven's Music* (Abingdon, 1995)."

2. "I am challenged by your question. If King's homiletical style and form are 'unique,' then to be 'effective today' implies that contemporary preachers who seek 'to move persons toward justice goals' should adopt or imitate his preaching. On the other hand, if to be 'effective today' means continuing to read and listen to King's own sermons in order to be reminded of what he stood for, then we must add the task of educating new generations of listeners as to who King was, what he was up against, and what he accomplished. I do believe that contemporary preachers should undertake the important work of proclaiming and practicing justice (see my new book, *Ministry at the Margins*, InterVarsity Press, 1997) and of helping people to understand the justice dimensions of the Christian gospel; but, in my opinion, we should be creative rather than imitative in our style and form of preaching."

Dr. Cheryl Sanders
Associate Professor
Christian Ethics
Howard University
Divinity School
Washington DC

IMPLICATIONS

My summation is that the legacy of Martin Luther King Jr.'s oration and theology of justice is very relevant still. Persons find, as did King, a unique biblical hermeneutic of justice that bears much authority. Much of the power of this authority is based not just on the biblical truth, but also is based on the power and form of delivery. We cannot escape the force of meaningful oratory of African American clergy, including King, that has given significant meaning to our understanding of Biblical mandates of love and justice.

NOTES

PREFACE

1. The "Invisible Institution" has reference to the worship and beliefs of Christianity maintained by slaves. It is called "Invisible" because slaves practiced Christian faith without the benefit of church physical buildings and their worship was often secret. See Edward Franklin Frazier, *The Negro Church in America* (New York: Schocken Books, 1963), chap. 2.

CHAPTER ONE

1. Drums are the most common and revered musical instruments in African culture. Traditionally, the drums vary in shape and size. The Yoruba motherdrum is large in size and produces a deep pitch. Among other types of drums is the hourglass-shaped tension drum known as the "talking drum." It can be used to imitate the tonal counters of spoken language. A smaller, tubular-shaped drum that produces a higher pitch is called the bembe. See Chris Waterman, "African Music," *Africana: The Encyclopedia of the African and the African Experience*, ed. Kwame Appiah and Henry Louis Gates (New York: Civitas Books, 1999), 1363–65.

2. Albert J. Raboteau, *A Fire in the Bones: Reflections on African-American Religious History* (Boston: Beacon Press, 1995), 17.

3. John S. Mbiti, *Introduction to African Religion* (Nairobi: East Africa Press, 1975), 10.

4. Ibid., 54–55.

5. Melva Wilson Costen, *African American Christian Worship* (Nashville, Tenn.: Abingdon Press, 1993), 104.

6. Edward Franklin Frazier, *The Negro Church in America* (New York: Schocken Books, 1963), 5.

7. Costen, *African American Christian Worship*, 38.

8. Henry H. Mitchell, "African American Preaching," *Concise Encyclopedia of Preaching*, ed. William H. Willimon and Richard Lischer (Louisville, Ky.: Westminster John Knox Press, 1995), 5.

9. *The Spirituals and the Blues: An Interpretation* [by] James H. Cone (New York: Seabury Press, 1972), 34.

10. David Emmanuel Goatley, *Were You There?: Godforsakenness in Slave Religion* (Maryknoll, N.Y.: Orbis Books, 1996), chap. 3.

11. Eileen Southern, *The Music of Black Americans: A History*, 2d ed. (New York: Norton, 1983), 546–47.

12. Ibid., 172.

13. Winthrop D. Jordan, *White Over Black: American Attitudes toward the Negro, 1550–1812* (Chapel Hill: University of North Carolina Press, 1968), chap 2.

14. Mitchell, *Black Preaching: The Recovery of a Powerful Art* (Nashville, Tenn.: Abingdon Press, 1990), 25.

15. Charles Joyner, "Believer I Know," *African-American Christianity: Essays in History*, ed. Paul E. Johnson (Berkeley: University of California Press, 1994), chap 2.

16. Dwight N. Hopkins, *Down, Up, and Over: Slave Religion and Black Theology* (Minneapolis: Fortress Press, 2000), 90.

17. Ibid., 92.

18. Edward D. Smith, *Climbing Jacob's Ladder: The Rise of Black Churches in Eastern American Cities, 1740–1877* (Washington: Smithsonian Institution Press, 1988), 26–27.

19. Mitchell, *Black Preaching*, 24.

20. Hymn written by John Newton (1725–1807) out of an experience of religious conversion. John left school at an early age and lived a life as a rough and wicked seaman. As a slave trader, he felt the deep fear of God and consequently trained for Christian ministry. The song expresses his joy that a "lost," "blind," and "wretch" of an individual as himself could experience God's grace. The hymn is a well-loved and cherished theological expression of African American religious ideals. For an in-depth story on Newton's life and the meaning of this and other hymns of the colonial era, see Kenneth W. Osbeck, *Amazing Grace* (Grand Rapids, Mich.: Kregel Publications, 1990).

21. Mitchell, *Black Preaching*, 27.

CHAPTER TWO

1. James H. Evans Jr., *We Have Been Believers: An African-American Systematic Theology* (Minneapolis: Fortress Press, 1992), 24.

2. Olin P. Moyd, *The Sacred Art: Preaching and Theology in the African American Tradition* (Valley Forge, Penn.: Judson Press, 1995), 34.

3. Eugene Lowry, "Narrative Preaching," *Concise Encyclopedia of Preaching*, ed. William H. Willimon and Richard Lischer (Louisville, Ky.: Westminster John Knox Press, 1995), 342.

4. Ibid.

5. Ibid., 343.

6. Sermon by Carolyn Ann Knight, "If Thou be a Great People," *The Heart of Black Preaching*, ed. Cleophus J. LaRue (Louisville, Ky.: Westminster John Knox Press, 2000), 227.

7. Vincent Wimbush, *Stony the Road We Trod: African American Biblical Interpretation*, ed. Cain Hope Felder (Minneapolis: Fortress Press, 1991), 82–83.

8. Henry H. Mitchell, *Black Preaching: The Recovery of a Powerful Art* (Nashville, Tenn.: Abingdon Press, 1990), 69.

9. Wyatt Tee Walker, *The Soul of Black Worship: A Trilogy—Preaching, Praying, Singing* (New York: Martin Luther King Fellows Press, 1984), 20.

10. LaRue, *The Heart of Black Preaching*, 20. LaRue also goes on to suggest that much of the authentication of the African American hermeneutical genres takes place in given "domains" of experience.

11. Thomas H. Troeger, *Imagining a Sermon* (Nashville, Tenn.: Abingdon Press, 1990), 26.

12. James H. Cone, *A Black Theology of Liberation*, twentieth anniversary ed. (Maryknoll, N. Y.: Orbis Books, 1990), xi.

13. James O. Stallings, *Telling the Story: Evangelism in Black Churches* (Valley Forge, Penn.: Judson Press, 1988), 92.

14. Qtd. in William B. McClain, *Come Sunday: The Liturgy of Zion* (Nashville, Tenn.: Abingdon Press, 1990), 64.

15. Paul Scott Wilson, *A Concise History of Preaching* (Nashville, Tenn.: Abingdon Press, 1992), 37–38.

16. Moyd, *The Sacred Art*, 58.

17. Melva Wilson Costen, *African American Christian Worship* (Nashville, Tenn.: Abingdon Press, 1993), 138.

18. Charles L. Campbell, "Inductive Preaching," *Concise Encyclopedia of Preaching*, 270.

19. Evans E. Crawford with Thomas H. Troeger, *The Hum: Call and Response in African American Preaching* (Nashville, Tenn.: Abingdon Press, 1995), 20.

20. LaRue, *The Heart of Black Preaching*, 69.

21. Mitchell, "African American Preaching," *Concise Encyclopedia of Preaching*, 5.

22. Ibid.

23. John Michael Spencer, "African American Folk Preaching," *Concise Encyclopedia of Preaching*, 143.

24. Walter F. Pitts, *Old Ship of Zion: The Afro-Baptist Ritual in the African Diaspora* (New York: Oxford University Press, 1993), 59.

25. Crawford, *The Hum*, 26.

26. Costen, *African American Christian Worship*, 105.

27. Crawford, *The Hum*, 26.

CHAPTER THREE

1. Coretta Scott King, ed., *The Words of Martin Luther King, Jr.* (New York: Newmarket Press, 1983), 52.

2. Keith D. Miller, *Voice of Deliverance: The Language of Martin Luther King, Jr., and Its Sources* (New York: Free Press, 1992), 18.

3. Sermon by King based on Luke 11:5–6 entitled, "A Knock at Midnight," in King's *Strength to Love* (New York: Harper & Row, [1963]), 66.

4. Lewis V. Baldwin, *To Make the Wounded Whole: The Cultural Legacy of Martin Luther King, Jr.* (Minneapolis: Fortress Press, 1992), 66.

5. Baldwin, "Martin Luther King, The Black Church, and the Black Messianic Vision," *Journal of the Interdenominational Theological Center* (fall 1984/spring 1985), 100.

6. King, "The Meaning of Hope," a sermon delivered on December 10, 1967, at the Dexter Avenue Baptist Church. Qtd. in Baldwin, *There is a Balm in Gilead: The Cultural Roots of Martin Luther King, Jr.* (Minneapolis: Fortress Press, 1991), 301–02.

7. Famed "I Have a Dream" speech, delivered by King during the March on Washington in August, 1963. Cited in James Melvin Washington, ed., *A Testament of Hope: The Essential Writings of Martin Luther King, Jr.* (San Francisco: Harper & Row, 1986), 217.

8. John Killinger, *Fundamentals of Preaching* (Philadelphia: Fortress Press, 1985), 55.

9. Ibid., 56.

10. King, *Strength to Love*, 127.

11. King, "The Answer to a Perplexing Question," *Strength to Love*, 132.

12. Ibid., 136.

13. Eugene Lowry, "Narrative Preaching," *Concise Encyclopedia of Preaching*, ed. William H. Willimon and Richard Lischer (Louisville, Ky.: Westminster John Knox Press, 1995), 342.

14. King, "Facing the Challenge of a New Age." This address was given during the First Annual Institute on Nonviolence and Social Change in December, 1956. Noted in Washington, *A Testament of Hope*, 144.

15. Lowry, "Narrative Preaching," 343.

16. King, "The Most Durable Power," a sermon that was given in November, 1956. It was delivered exactly a week prior to the victorious Supreme Court ruling that ended the Montgomery bus boycott. Text is cited in Washington, *A Testament of Hope*, 10.

17. Garth Baker-Fletcher, *Somebodyness: Martin Luther King, Jr., and the Theory of Dignity* (Minneapolis: Fortress Press, 1993), 36.

18. Carl H. Marbury, "Biblical and Theological Rhetoric of King," *Martin Luther King, Jr.: Civil Rights Leader, Theologian, Orator*, vol. 3, ed. David J. Garrow (Brooklyn, N.Y.: Carlson Publishing, 1989), 625–26.

19. Donald K. McKim, *The Bible in Theology and Preaching: A Theological Guide for Preaching* (Nashville, Tenn.: Abingdon Press, 1994), 128–29.

20. King, "Where Do We Go From Here?" This address carried an even deeper significance in that it was King's last presidential address to the Southern Christian Leadership Conference. Cited in Washington, *A Testament of Hope*, 251.

21. G. M. Tucker, "Traditions and Theology of Care in the Old Testament and Apocrypha," *Dictionary of Pastoral Care and Counseling*, ed. Rodney Hunter (Nashville, Tenn.: Abingdon Press, 1990), 806.

22. Richard Lischer, *The Preacher King: Martin Luther King, Jr. and the Word that Moved America* (New York: Oxford University Press, 1995), 213.

23. King, "The Death of Evil upon the Seashore," *Strength to Love*, 79.

24. Henry H. Mitchell, *Black Preaching: The Recovery of a Powerful Art* (Nashville: Tenn.: Abingdon Press, 1990), 59.

25. King, "I See the Promised Land" (a.k.a. "I've Been to the Mountaintop"). This was King's very last sermon. The emotional and mysterious homily was given at the Mason Temple in Memphis just hours before the twentieth-century prophet mortally fell to an assassin's bullet. The speech is cited in Washington, *A Testament of Hope*, 286.

26. Ibid., 218.

27. Walter J. Burghardt, *Preaching: The Art and the Craft* (New York: Paulist Press, 1987), 143.

28. See O. C. Edwards Jr., "A History of Preaching," *Concise Encyclopedia of Preaching*, 216.

29. James H. Cone, *Malcolm and Martin and America: A Dream or a Nightmare?* (Maryknoll, N.Y.: Orbis Books, 1991), 62.

30. Ibid., 63.

31. King in a sermon entitled, "Loving Your Enemies," *Strength to Love*, 56.

32. Ibid., 57.

33. William D. Watley, *Roots of Resistance: The Nonviolent Ethic of Martin Luther King, Jr.* (Valley Forge, Penn.: Judson Press, 1985), 50–51.

34. Cone, *Malcolm and Martin and America*, 127.

35. Paul Scott Wilson. "Imagination," *Concise Encyclopedia of Preaching*, 267.

36. Sermon by King based on Matthew 10:16 entitled "A Tough Mind and a Tender Heart," *Strength to Love*, 20.

37. King, "Where Do We Go From Here?" *A Testament of Hope*, 252.

38. Walter Brueggemann, *The Prophetic Imagination* (Philadelphia: Fortress Press, 1978), 13.

39. Enoch H. Oglesby, *Clues from God's Divine Arithmetic: Christian Ethics for Preaching and Evangelism* (Nashville, Tenn.: Townsend Press, 1985), 59.

40. Qtd. in *I Have a Dream: Writings and Speeches that Changed the World/ Martin Luther King, Jr.*, ed. James Melvin Washington (San Francisco: HarperSanFrancisco, 1992), 122–23.

41. King, "Birth of a New Nation," as cited in Clayborne Carson, *The Autobiography of Martin Luther King, Jr.* (New York: Warner Books, 1998), 112–13.

42. Ibid., 113.

43. Evans E. Crawford with Thomas H. Troeger, *The Hum: Call and Response in African American Preaching* (Nashville, Tenn.: Abingdon Press, 1995), 52–53.

44. Troeger, "Figures of Speech," *Concise Encyclopedia of Preaching*, 123.

45. King, *Strength to Love*, 67–68.

46. Martha Solomon, "Covenanted Rights: The Metaphorical Matrix of 'I Have A Dream,'" *Martin Luther King, Jr., and the Sermonic Power of Public Discourse*, ed. Carolyn Calloway-Thomas and John Louis Lucaites (Tuscaloosa: University of Alabama Press, 1993), 69.

47. King, "Death of Evil upon the Seashore," *Strength to Love*, 85–86.

48. Mitchell, *Celebration and Experience in Preaching* (Nashville, Tenn.: Abingdon Press, 1990), 44.

49. David Buttrick, *Homiletic: Moves and Structures* (Philadelphia: Fortress Press, 1987), 122.

50. Robert Harrison and Linda Harrison, "The Call From the Mountaintop: Call-Response and the Oratory of Martin Luther King, Jr.," *Martin Luther King, Jr., and the Sermonic Power of Public Discourse*, 169.

51. Lischer, *The Preacher King*, 128–29.

52. King, "I See the Promised Land," *A Testament of Hope*, 286.

53. King, "I Have a Dream," *The Autobiography of Martin Luther King, Jr.*, 223–25.

54. Cornel West, "The Religious Foundations of the Thought of Martin Luther King, Jr." *We Shall Overcome: Martin Luther King, Jr., and the Black Freedom Struggle*, ed. Peter J. Albert and Ronald Hoffman (New York: Da Capo Press, 1993), 122–23.

55. Samuel D. Proctor, *The Certain Sound of the Trumpet: Crafting a Sermon of Authority* (Valley Forge, Penn.: Judson Press, 1994), 77.

CHAPTER FOUR

1. Henry H. Mitchell intentionally uses the title in *Celebration and Experience in Preaching* (Nashville, Tenn.: Abingdon Press, 1990), 132.

2. Frank A. Thomas, *They Like to Never Quit Praisin' God: The Role of Celebration in Preaching* (Cleveland: United Church Press, 1997), 31.

3. Ibid., 18.

4. David Buttrick, *Homiletic: Moves and Structures* (Philadelphia: Fortress Press, 1987), 226.

5. Ibid., 233–34.

6. Gardner C. Taylor, "At Year's End" (sermon delivered on December 28, 1969), *The Words of Gardner Taylor*, ed. Edward L. Taylor (Valley Forge, Penn.: Judson Press, 1999), 107.

7. John S. Mbiti, *Introduction to African Religion* (Nairobi: East Africa Press, 1975), 174–75.

8. David Shannon, "An Antebellum Sermon," *Stony the Road We Trod: African American Biblical Interpretation*, ed. Cain Hope Felder (Minneapolis: Fortress Press, 1991), 112.

9. James M. Childs Jr., *Preaching Justice: The Ethical Vocation of Word and Sacrament Ministry* (Harrisburg, Penn.: Trinity Press International, 2000), 41.

10. Enoch H. Oglesby, *Ethics and Theology from the Other Side* (Washington: University Press, 1979), 35.

11. Stephen Breek Reid, "The African American Scholar between Text and People," *Cross Currents* 44 (winter 1994/1995), 479.

12. Mitchell, *Black Preaching: The Recovery of a Powerful Art* (Nashville, Tenn.: Abingdon Press, 1990), 20–21.

13. Gary V. Simpson, "Preaching by Punctuation," *The Courage to Hope, From Black Suffering to Human Redemption: Essays in Honor of James Melvin Washington*, ed. Quinton Hosford Dixie and Cornel West (Boston, Mass.: Beacon Press, 1999), 153–55.

14. Robert M. Franklin, *Another Day's Journey: Black Churches Confronting the American Crisis* (Minneapolis: Fortress Press, 1997), 69.

15. Ibid., 15.

16. Enoch H. Oglesby, *O Lord, Move this Mountain: Racism and Christian Ethics* (St. Louis, Mo.: Chalice Press, 1998), 62. In addition to lines of direction and explanation of each stage of moral decision making, Oglesby also provides very careful and distinct scriptural references that enhance the intent and theology of each given stage.

17. James H. Cone, *Risks of Faith: The Emergence of a Black Theology of Liberation, 1968–1998* (Boston, Mass.: Beacon Press, 1999), 78–79.

18. For in-depth biographies of historical African American female clergy journeys, see, for example, Judith Weisenfeld and Richard Newman, eds., *This Far by Faith: Readings in African-American Women's Religious Biography* (New York: Routledge, 1996).

CHAPTER FIVE

1. Samuel D. Proctor, *"How Shall They Hear?": Effective Preaching for Vital Faith* (Valley Forge, Penn.: Judson Press, 1992), 38.

2. Dwight N. Hopkins, *Shoes that Fit Our Feet: Sources for a Constructive Black Theology,* (Maryknoll, N. Y.: Orbis Books, 1993), 203.

3. James H. Harris, *Preaching Liberation* (Minneapolis: Fortress Press, 1995), 63.

4. Henry H. Mitchell, *Celebration and Experience in Preaching* (Nashville, Tenn.: Abingdon Press, 1990), 20.

5. Richard M. Gula, *What Are They Saying about Moral Norms?* (New York: Paulist Press, 1982), 110.

6. Quoted in Arthur Van Seters, ed., *Preaching as a Social Act: Theology and Practice* (Nashville, Tenn.: Abingdon Press, 1988), 206.

7. Ibid., 207.

EPILOGUE

1. James H. Cone, *Risks of Faith: The Emergence of a Black Theology of Liberation, 1968–1998* (Boston, Mass.: Beacon Press, 1999), 62.

BIBLIOGRAPHY

Achtemeier, Elizabeth. *Preaching as Theology and Art.* Nashville, Tenn.: Abingdon Press, 1984.

Adamiak, Richard. *Justice and History in the Old Testament: The Evolution of Divine Retribution in the Historiographies of the Wilderness Generation.* Cleveland, Oh.: J. T. Zubal, 1982.

Albert, Peter J., and Ronald Hoffman, eds. *We Shall Overcome: Martin Luther King, Jr., and the Black Freedom Struggle.* New York: Da Capo Press, 1993.

Ansbro, John J. *Martin Luther King, Jr.: The Making of a Mind.* Maryknoll, N.Y.: Orbis Books, 1982.

Apel, William. *Silent Conversations: Reading the Bible in Good Company.* Valley Forge, Penn.: Judson Press, 2000.

Baker, Houston A., Jr. *Black Studies, Rap, and the Academy.* Chicago: University of Chicago Press, 1993.

Baker-Fletcher, Garth. *Somebodyness: Martin Luther King, Jr., and the Theory of Dignity.* Minneapolis: Fortress Press, 1993.

Baldwin, Lewis V. "Martin Luther King, The Black Church, and the Black Messianic Vision." *Journal of the Interdenominational Theological Center* (fall 1984/spring 1985): 93–108.

———. *There is a Balm in Gilead: The Cultural Roots of Martin Luther King, Jr.* Minneapolis: Fortress Press, 1991.

———. *To Make the Wounded Whole: The Cultural Legacy of Martin Luther King, Jr.* Minneapolis: Fortress Press, 1992.

Bennett, Lerone. *What Manner of Man; A Biography of Martin Luther King, Jr.* Chicago: Johnson Publishing, 1964.

Birch, Bruce C. *Let Justice Roll Down: The Old Testament, Ethics, and Christian Life.* Louisville, Ky.: Westminster John Knox Press, 1991.

Branch, Taylor. *Parting the Waters: America in the King Years, 1954–63.* New York: Simon and Schuster, 1988.

Brueggemann, Walter. *Hopeful Imagination: Prophetic Voices in Exile.* Philadelphia: Fortress Press, 1986.

——. *The Prophetic Imagination.* Philadelphia: Fortress Press, 1978.

Burghardt, Walter J. *Preaching: The Art and the Craft.* New York: Paulist Press, 1987.

Buttrick, David. *Homiletic: Moves and Structures.* Philadelphia: Fortress Press, 1987.

Calloway-Thomas, Carolyn, and John Louis Lucaites, eds. *Martin Luther King, Jr., and the Sermonic Power of Public Discourse.* Tuscaloosa: University of Alabama Press, 1993.

Carson, Clayborne, ed. *The Autobiography of Martin Luther King, Jr.* New York: Intellectual Properties Management/Warner Books, 1998.

Carson, Clayborne, and Peter Holloran, eds. *A Knock at Midnight: Inspiration from the Great Sermons of Reverend Martin Luther King, Jr.* New York: Intellectual Properties Management/Warner Books, 1998.

Childs, James M., Jr. *Preaching Justice: The Ethical Vocation of Word and Sacrament Ministry.* Harrisburg, Penn.: Trinity Press, 2000.

Chinula, Donald M. *Building King's Beloved Community: Foundations for Pastoral Care and Counseling with the Oppressed.* Cleveland: United Church Press, 1997.

Collier-Thomas, Bettye. *Daughters of Thunder: Black Women Preachers and their Sermons, 1850–1979.* San Francisco: Jossey-Bass Publishers, 1998.

Cone, James H. *A Black Theology of Liberation.* Twentieth anniversary ed. Maryknoll, N.Y.: Orbis Books, 1990.

——. *For My People: Black Theology and the Black Church.* Maryknoll, N.Y.: Orbis Books, 1984.

——. *Malcolm and Martin and America: A Dream or a Nightmare?* Maryknoll, N.Y.: Orbis Books, 1991.

——. *Risks of Faith: The Emergence of a Black Theology of Liberation, 1968–1998.* Boston, Mass.: Beacon Press, 1999.

———. *The Spirituals and the Blues: An Interpretation [by] James H. Cone.* New York: Seabury Press, 1972.

Cooper-Lewter, Nicholas C., and Henry H. Mitchell. *Soul Theology: The Heart of American Black Culture.* San Francisco: Harper & Row, 1986.

Costen, Melva Wilson. *African American Christian Worship.* Nashville, Tenn.: Abingdon Press, 1993.

Craddock, Fred B. *Overhearing the Gospel.* Nashville, Tenn.: Abingdon Press, 1978.

Crawford, Evans E., with Thomas H. Troeger. *The Hum: Call and Response in African American Preaching.* Nashville, Tenn.: Abingdon Press, 1995.

Dixie, Quinton Hosford, and Cornel West, eds. *The Courage to Hope: From Black Suffering to Human Redemption: Essays in Honor of James Melvin Washington.* Boston: Beacon Press, 1999.

Dyson, Michael Eric. *I May Not Get There with You: The True Martin Luther King, Jr.* New York: Free Press, 2000.

Elliott, Mark Barger. *Creative Styles of Preaching.* Louisville, Ky.: Westminster John Knox Press, 2000.

Evans, James H., Jr. *We Have Been Believers: An African-American Systematic Theology.* Minneapolis: Fortress Press, 1992.

Felder, Cain Hope, ed. *Stony the Road We Trod: African American Biblical Interpretation.* Minneapolis: Fortress Press, 1991.

Franklin, Robert M. *Another Day's Journey: Black Churches Confronting the American Crisis.* Minneapolis: Fortress Press, 1997.

Frazier, Edward Franklin. *The Negro Church in America.* New York: Schocken Books, 1963.

Garrow, David J. *Bearing the Cross: Martin Luther King, Jr., and the Southern Christian Leadership Conference.* New York: Morrow, 1986.

———, ed. *Martin Luther King, Jr.: Civil Rights Leader, Theologian, Orator.* 3 vols. Brooklyn, N.Y.: Carlson Publishing, 1989.

Goatley, David Emmanuel. *Were You There?: Godforsakenness in Slave Religion.* Maryknoll, N.Y.: Orbis Books, 1996.

Gula, Richard M. *What Are They Saying about Moral Norms?* New York: Paulist Press, 1982.

Harding, Vincent. *Martin Luther King, the Inconvenient Hero.* Maryknoll, N.Y.: Orbis Books, 1996.

Harris, James H. *Preaching Liberation*. Minneapolis: Fortress Press, 1995.

Hopkins, Dwight N., ed. *Black Faith and Public Talk: Critical Essays on James H. Cone's Black Theology and Black Power*. Maryknoll, N.Y.: Orbis Books, 1999.

———. *Down, Up, and Over: Slave Religion and Black Theology*. Minneapolis: Fortress Press, 2000.

———. *Shoes That Fit Our Feet: Sources for a Constructive Black Theology*. Maryknoll, N.Y.: Orbis Books, 1993.

Hunter, Rodney, ed. *Dictionary of Pastoral Care and Counseling*. Nashville, Tenn.: Abingdon Press, 1990.

Johnson, Paul E., ed. *African-American Christianity: Essays in History*. Berkeley: University of California Press, 1994.

Jordan, R. L. *Black Theology Exposed*. New York: Vantage Press, 1982.

Jordan, Winthrop D. *White over Black: American Attitudes toward the Negro, 1550–1812*. Chapel Hill: University of North Carolina Press, 1968.

Killinger, John. *Fundamentals of Preaching*. Philadelphia: Fortress Press, 1985.

King, Coretta Scott. *My Life with Martin Luther King, Jr.* New York: Holt, Rinehart, & Winston, 1969.

———, ed. *The Words of Martin Luther King, Jr.* New York: Newmarket Press, 1983.

King, Martin Luther, Jr. *Strength to Love*. New York: Harper & Row, [1963].

———. *Where Do We Go From Here: Chaos or Community?* New York: Harper & Row, [1967].

———. *Why We Can't Wait*. New York: Harper & Row, [1964].

LaRue, Cleophus J. *The Heart of Black Preaching*. Louisville, Ky.: Westminster John Knox Press, 2000.

Lincoln, C. Eric, ed. *Martin Luther King, Jr.: A Profile*. New York: Hill and Wang, [1970].

Lischer, Richard. *The Preacher King: Martin Luther King, Jr. and the Word that Moved America*. New York: Oxford University Press, 1995.

Massey, James Earl. *Designing a Sermon: Order and Movement in Preaching*. Nashville, Tenn.: Abingdon Press, 1980.

Mbiti, John S. *Introduction to African Religion*. Nairobi: East Africa Press, 1975.

McClain, William B. *Come Sunday: The Liturgy of Zion*. Nashville, Tenn.: Abingdon Press, 1990.

McKenzie, Vashti M. *Not without a Struggle: Leadership Development for African American Women in Ministry*. Cleveland: United Church Press, 1996.

McKim, Donald K. *The Bible in Theology and Preaching: A Theological Guide for Preaching*. Nashville, Tenn.: Abingdon Press, 1994.

McMickle, Marvin A. *Preaching to the Black Middle Class: Words of Challenge, Words of Hope*. Valley Forge, Penn.: Judson Press, 2000.

Miller, Keith D. *Voice of Deliverance: The Language of Martin Luther King, Jr., and Its Sources*. New York: Free Press, 1992.

Mitchell, Henry H. *Black Preaching: The Recovery of a Powerful Art*. Nashville, Tenn.: Abingdon Press, 1990.

———. *Celebration and Experience in Preaching*. Nashville, Tenn.: Abingdon Press, 1990

Moyd, Olin P. *Redemption in Black Theology*. Valley Forge, Penn.: Judson Press, 1979.

———. *The Sacred Art: Preaching and Theology in the African American Tradition*. Valley Forge, Penn.: Judson Press, 1995.

O'Day, Gail R., and Thomas G. Long, eds. *Listening to the Word: Studies in Honor of Fred B. Craddock*. Nashville, Tenn.: Abingdon Press, 1993.

Oglesby, Enoch H. *Clues from God's Divine Arithmetic: Christian Ethics for Preaching and Evangelism*. Nashville, Tenn.: Townsend Press, 1985.

———. *Ethics and Theology from the Other Side: Sounds of Moral Struggle*. Washington: University Press of America, 1979.

———. "Martin Luther King, Jr.: Liberation in a Christian Context." *Interdenominational Theological Center Journal* (spring 1977): 33–41.

———. *O Lord, Move this Mountain: Racism and Christian Ethics*. St. Louis, Mo.: Chalice Press, 1998.

Paris, Peter J. *Black Leaders in Conflict: Joseph H. Jackson, Martin Luther King, Jr., Malcolm X, Adam Clayton Powell, Jr*. New York: The Pilgrim Press, 1978.

——. *The Social Teaching of the Black Churches.* Philadelphia: Fortress Press, 1985.

Pitts, Walter F. *Old Ship of Zion: The Afro-Baptist Ritual in the African Diaspora.* New York: Oxford University Press, 1993.

Proctor, Samuel D. *The Certain Sound of the Trumpet: Crafting a Sermon of Authority.* Valley Forge, Penn.: Judson Press, 1994.

——. *"How Shall They Hear?": Effective Preaching for Vital Faith.* Valley Forge, Penn.: Judson Press, 1992.

Raboteau, Albert J. *A Fire in the Bones: Reflections on African-American Religious History.* Boston: Beacon Press, 1995.

Reid, Stephen Breek. "The African American Scholar between Text and People." *Cross Currents* 44 (winter 94/95): 476–88.

Roberts, J. Deotis. *A Black Political Theology.* Philadelphia: Westminster Press, [1974].

Schubeck, Thomas L. *Liberation Ethics: Sources, Models, and Norms.* Minneapolis: Fortress Press, 1993.

Smith, Edward D. *Climbing Jacob's Ladder: The Rise of Black Churches in Eastern American Cities, 1740–1877.* Washington: Smithsonian Institution Press, 1988.

Smith, Kelly Miller. *Social Crisis Preaching.* Macon, Ga: Mercer University Press, 1984.

Southern, Eileen. *The Music of Black Americans: A History.* 2d ed. New York: Norton, 1983.

Spencer, Jon Michael. *Black Hymnody: A Hymnological History of the African-American Church.* Knoxville: University of Tennessee Press, 1992.

——. *Sing a New Song: Liberating Black Hymnody.* Minneapolis: Fortress Press, 1995.

Stallings, James O. *Telling the Story: Evangelism in Black Churches.* Valley Forge, Penn.: Judson Press, 1988.

Taylor, Gardner. *The Words of Gardner Taylor.* Ed. Edward L. Taylor. Valley Forge, Penn.: Judson Press, 1999.

Thomas, Frank A. *They Like to Never Quit Praisin' God: The Role of Celebration in Preaching.* Cleveland: United Church Press, 1997.

Thurman, Howard. *Jesus and the Disinherited.* New York: Abingdon-Cokesbury Press, [1949].

Tillich, Paul. *The Courage to Be.* New Haven: Yale University Press, 1952.

——. *The Shaking of the Foundations [Sermons]*. New York: C. Scribner's Sons, 1948.

Trimiew, Darryl M. *Voices of the Silenced: The Responsible Self in a Marginalized Community*. Cleveland: The Pilgrim Press, 1993.

Troeger, Thomas H. *Imagining a Sermon*. Nashville, Tenn.: Abingdon Press, 1990.

Tutu, Mpilo Desmond. *Hope and Suffering: Sermons and Speeches*. Grand Rapids, Mich.: W. B. Eerdmans, 1983.

Van Seters, Arthur, ed. *Preaching as a Social Act: Theology and Practice*. Nashville, Tenn.: Abingdon Press, 1988.

Walker, Wyatt Tee. *"Somebody's Calling My Name": Black Sacred Music and Social Change*. Valley Forge, Penn.: Judson Press, 1979.

——. *The Soul of Black Worship: A Trilogy—Preaching, Praying, Singing*. New York: Martin Luther King Fellows Press, 1984.

Washington, James Melvin, ed. *Conversations with God: Two Centuries of Prayers by African-Americans*. New York: HarperCollins Publishers, 1994.

——. *I Have a Dream: Writings and Speeches that Changed the World/ Martin Luther King, Jr*. San Francisco: HarperSanFrancisco, 1992.

——. *A Testament of Hope: The Essential Writings of Martin Luther King, Jr*. San Francisco: Harper & Row, 1986.

Watley, William D. *Roots of Resistance: The Nonviolent Ethic of Martin Luther King, Jr*. Valley Forge, Penn.: Judson Press, 1985.

Westermann, Claus. *Basic Forms of Prophetic Speech*. Trans. Hugh Clayton White. Cambridge: Lutherworth Press, 1991.

Willimon, William H., and Richard Lischer, eds. *Concise Encyclopedia of Preaching*. Louisville, Ky.: Westminster John Knox Press, 1995.

Wilson, Paul Scott. *A Concise History of Preaching*. Nashville, Tenn.: Abingdon Press, 1992.

Wimbush, Vincent L., ed. *African Americans and the Bible: Sacred Texts and Social Textures*. New York: Continuum Press, 2000.

Young, Henry J. *Major Black Religious Leaders, 1775–1940*. Nashville, Tenn.: Abingdon Press, 1977.